Ready-to-Use

VOCABULARY, WORD ANALYSIS & COMPREHENSION ACTIVITIES

First Grade Reading Level

HENRIETTE L. ALLEN, Ph.D.
WALTER B. BARBE, Ph.D.
LINDA LEHNER

THE CENTER FOR APPLIED
RESEARCH IN EDUCATION
West Nyack, New York 10994

Library of Congress Cataloging-in-Publication Data

Allen, Henriette L.
  Ready-to-use vocabulary, word analysis & comprehension activities
  Henriette L. Allen, Walter B. Barbe, Linda Lehner.
    p.   cm. — (Reading skills activities library)
  Contents: [1] First grade reading level — [2] Second grade
reading level — [3] Third grade reading level.
    ISBN 0-87628-932-4 (v. 1). — ISBN 0-87628-933-2 (v. 2). — ISBN
0-87628-934-0 (v. 3)
    1. Reading (Elementary)—Problems, exercises, etc.   2. Reading
comprehension—Problems, exercises, etc.   3. Vocabulary—Study and
teaching (Elementary)—Problems, exercises, etc.   I. Barbe, Walter
Burke, 1926–   II. Lehner, Linda.   III. Title.   IV. Series.
LB1573.A44   1996
372.4—dc20   96-18332
                                                          CIP

© 1996 *by* The Center for Applied Research in Education, West Nyack, NY

Printed in the United States of America

10 9 8 7 6 5 4 3 2

ISBN 0-87628-932-4

ATTENTION: CORPORATIONS AND SCHOOLS

The Center for Applied Research in Education books are available at quantity discounts with bulk purchase for educational, business, or sales promotional use. For information, please write to Prentice Hall Special Sales, 240 Frisch Court, Paramus, NJ 07652. Please supply: title of book, ISBN number, quantity, how the book will be used, date needed.

**THE CENTER FOR APPLIED RESEARCH
IN EDUCATION**
West Nyack, NY 10994

On the World Wide Web at http://www.phdirect.com

Prentice-Hall International (UK) Limited, *London*
Prentice-Hall of Australia Pty. Limited, *Sydney*
Prentice-Hall Canada Inc., *Toronto*
Prentice-Hall Hispanoamaricana, S.A., *Mexico*
Prentice-Hall of India Private Limited, *New Delhi*
Prentice-Hall of Japan, Inc., *Tokyo*
Pearson Education Asia Pte. Ltd., *Singapore*
Editora Prentice-Hall do Brazil, Ltda., *Rio de Janeiro*

About the
READING SKILLS
ACTIVITIES LIBRARY

The "Reading Skills Activities Library" is designed to give classroom teachers, reading specialists, and others who teach reading multiple learning activities to build specific reading skills at each grade level, first through third grade. Each grade level unit provides 200 or more reproducible reading and writing activities to help children master reading skills that can be used with *any* reading program.

FIRST LEVEL   *Ready-to-Use Vocabulary, Word Analysis & Comprehension Activities—FIRST GRADE READING LEVEL*

SECOND LEVEL   *Ready-to-Use Vocabulary, Word Analysis & Comprehension Activities—SECOND GRADE READING LEVEL*

THIRD LEVEL   *Ready-to-Use Vocabulary, Word Analysis & Comprehension Activities—THIRD GRADE READING LEVEL*

The skill activities follow the sequence in the Reading Skills Check Lists developed by nationally known educator Walter B. Barbe, Ph.D. The activities can be assigned to individuals or groups and supervised by the teacher, a paraprofessional, a parent, a volunteer, or a peer.

Each grade level unit of Reading Skills Activities includes:

1. Directions for using the reading activities at that level to support direct instruction
2. At least 200 reproducible activities for quick, reliable practice or enrichment of each reading skill, with answer keys at the end
3. A reproducible Reading Skills Check List for the major skill areas covered at that level for easy individual or group recordkeeping

You will find that the "Reading Skills Activities Library" provides for:

- Quick, accurate prescriptive help to meet specific reading needs
- A minimum of four ready-to-use reading skills exercises to reinforce, supplement, and enrich instruction in each skill
- Flexibility in planning individual and group activities, homework assignments, and peer- or aide-assisted instruction

The activities can be used by the teacher, parent, or reading specialist in any learning setting, in any manner the teacher deems most appropriate. They are meant to provide handy, efficient, systematic help in developing reading skills that students need to become proficient readers.

Henriette L. Allen
Walter B. Barbe

About the Authors

Henriette L. Allen, Ph.D.

Henriette L. Allen, Ph.D., is a former classroom teacher in the schools of Coventry, Rhode Island, the Aramco Schools of Dhahran, Saudi Arabia, The American Community School of Benghazi, Libya, and Jackson, Mississippi. Dr. Allen served in several administrative roles, including assistant superintendent of the Jackson Public Schools. She is presently an education consultant recognized nationally. Dr. Allen is the senior author of the series *Competency Tests for Basic Reading Skills* (West Nyack, NY: The Center for Applied Research in Education.) She has taught reading skills at both elementary and secondary levels, has supervised the development of a Continuous Progress Reading Program for the Jackson Public Schools, and has lectured widely in the fields of reading, classroom management, technology in the classroom, and leadership in educational administration. Dr. Allen is listed in the *World Who's Who of Women* and *Who's Who—School District Officials*. She was the 1996 recipient of the Distinguished Service Award given by the American Association of School Administrators.

Walter B. Barbe, Ph.D.

A nationally known authority in the fields of reading and learning disabilities, Walter B. Barbe, Ph.D., was for twenty-five years editor-in-chief of the widely acclaimed magazine *Highlights for Children*, and adjunct professor at The Ohio State University. Dr. Barbe is the author of over 150 professional articles and a number of books, including *Personalized Reading Instruction* (West Nyack, NY: Parker Publishing Company, Inc.), coauthoried with Jerry L. Abbot. He is also the senior author and editor of two series—*Creative Growth with Handwriting* (Columbus, OH: Zaner-Bloser, Inc.) and *Barbe Reading Skills Check Lists and Activities* (West Nyack, NY: The Center for Applied Research in Education, Inc.)—and he is senior editor of *Competency Tests for Basic Reading Skills*. Dr. Barbe is a fellow of the American Psychological Association and is listed in *Who's Who in America* and *American Men of Science*.

Linda Lehner, M.Ed.

Linda Lehner, M.Ed., has taught reading at both the primary and intermediate grade levels and successfully piloted an Early Childhood Education program with parent involvement in Jackson, Mississippi. The program has received national recognition and has been used as a model for similar programs across the country. Mrs. Lehner has given many workshops on Early Childhood Education and Parent Involvement throughout the United States. She was selected for a "Teacher Best Promoting Community" award in 1976.

Contents

• **VOCABULARY**

    A. Word Recognition • 17
        1. Recognizes Words with Both Upper- and Lower-Case Letters at
            Beginning • 17–22
        2. Knows Names of Letters in Sequence • 23–29
        3. Is Able to Identify in Various Settings the Following Words Usually Found
            in Preprimers and Primers • 30–53

____ a	____ by	____ fine	____ house	____ mother
____ about	____ cake	____ fish	____ how	____ must
____ again	____ call	____ for	____ I	____ my
____ all	____ came	____ from	____ if	____ near
____ am	____ can	____ fun	____ in	____ new
____ an	____ car	____ funny	____ is	____ night
____ and	____ Christmas	____ get	____ it	____ no
____ apple	____ come	____ girl	____ jump	____ not
____ are	____ cookies	____ give	____ just	____ of
____ as	____ could	____ go	____ kitten	____ on
____ at	____ cow	____ good	____ know	____ one
____ away	____ cowboy	____ good-by	____ laugh	____ or
____ baby	____ daddy	____ green	____ let	____ party
____ back	____ day	____ had	____ like	____ pie
____ ball	____ did	____ happy	____ little	____ play
____ be	____ dinner	____ has	____ long	____ pretty
____ bed	____ dish	____ have	____ look	____ puppy
____ been	____ do	____ he	____ make	____ put
____ big	____ dog	____ help	____ man	____ rabbit
____ birthday	____ down	____ her	____ many	____ ran
____ black	____ eat	____ here	____ may	____ red
____ blue	____ farm	____ hide	____ me	____ ride
____ boat	____ fast	____ him	____ mitten	____ run
____ boy	____ father	____ his	____ more	____ said
____ but	____ find	____ home	____ morning	____ sat

Contents

____ saw
____ see
____ she
____ show
____ sleep
____ so
____ some
____ something
____ soon
____ splash
____ stop

____ surprise
____ table
____ take
____ thank
____ that
____ the
____ their
____ them
____ then
____ there
____ they

____ this
____ to
____ too
____ toy
____ tree
____ TV
____ two
____ up
____ us
____ walk
____ want

____ was
____ water
____ way
____ we
____ went
____ were
____ what
____ when
____ where
____ which
____ white

____ who
____ will
____ wish
____ with
____ woman
____ work
____ would
____ yellow
____ yes
____ you
____ your

• **COMPREHENSION**

Contents

How to Use These
Reading Skills Activities
Most Effectively

The learning activities in this unit can help you make optimal use of time in helping each of your students learn to read. The first requirement for a positive learning situation is, of course, your own enthusiastic teaching. Nothing replaces that. However, the student must apply what has been taught. Instruction must be followed through. Practice is needed in order to be sure that a skill has not only been learned but mastered.

In order for skills to develop sequentially, it is vital that you know where a student is within the sequence of reading skills. The Reading Skills Check List and practice activities in this unit provide a practical and systematic means to meet the specific reading skill needs of each of your pupils on a continuing, day-to-day basis.

The reading activities offer ready-to-use opportunities to learn, practice and master the vocabulary, word analysis, and comprehension skills at the first grade level, including at least four pages of practice work directed to each skill. Each activity is tailored to meet the learning needs of students at the first grade level. The activities provide complete, easy-to-follow student directions and may be duplicated as many times as needed for individual or group use. Complete answer keys are provided at the end of the unit.

The Reading Skills Check List is *not* intended as a rigid instructional program. Rather, it is meant to offer a general pattern around which a program may be built. The check list may be used to verify (1) where the student is in a sequence of reading skills, (2) when the student masters the skills, and (3) the number of skills mastered.

A copy of the Reading Skills Check List: FIRST LEVEL is on pages 12–13 for your optional use.

IDENTIFYING INDIVIDUAL READING NEEDS

Before planning an instructional program for any pupil, it is necessary to determine at what level the student is reading. This may be accomplished through the use of an informal reading inventory. Many such informal assessment devices are provided in *Alternative Assessment Techniques for Reading & Writing* (West Nyack, NY: The Center for Applied Research in Education, 1996), by Wilma H. Miller.

Once a pupil's areas of difficulty are identified, instruction can then be planned, taught, and reinforced through practice. When the student has worked through a unit of instruction, a posttest to verify mastery of the skill may be given. When mastery occurs, the student progresses to another skill. When the student is unsuccessful in a specific reading skill and a reasonable amount of instruction does not result in mastery, it may be that a different instructional method or approach is needed, or a preliminary skill needs reevaluation followed by additional teaching–learning activities.

TEACHING AND REINFORCING SKILLS

After a reading skill has been identified as lacking, the teaching-learning process begins. The skill may be taught using the basal reader, selected children's literature, and/or your reading program as the basic source of information. Explaining the skill, giving the rules which apply, and illustrating by examples are frequently used techniques. The next step in the teaching-learning process is to assign an activity with which the student can try his or her wings at learning. The activity indicates if the learning has occurred or verifies that the student understands the lesson. When the student meets that particular situation in a reading selection, he or she can apply the appropriate reading skill.

At this point in the learning process, the reading skills activities should become a valuable teaching asset. They include several pages of practice exercises for every reading objective on the reading skills check list as well as those found in every reading program. You can select the exercises specifically designed to aid students at their particular level of reading development. After the paper-and-pencil activities are completed—during class time, as a homework assignment, as a cooperative learning activity or a peer instruction activity—results of the learning activity should be discussed with the student. You can then prescribe additional practice for the skill, reteach the skill, or proceed to the next activity.

RECORDKEEPING ON THE SKILLS CHECK LIST

Recordkeeping is an important part of any instructional design. Simplicity and ease are vital. One suggested method for marking the skills check list is as follows.

B. Structural Analysis
  1. Knows endings
      a. *ed* sound as "ed" in *wanted*
      b. *ed* sound as "d" in *moved*
      c. *ed* sound as "t" in *liked*
  2. Recognizes compound words (*into, upon*)
  3. Knows common word families

all ___	an ___	ell ___	ook ___	in ___
it ___	ill ___	ay ___	ing ___	ish ___
it ___	et ___	ake ___	ack ___	ight ___

C. Word Form Clues
  1. Recognizes upper- and lower-case letters

M		
8/20	M	8/28
M		

Put an *M* in the first column if the pupil takes a test and demonstrates mastery of that basic reading skill. If the pupil has not mastered the skill, record the date. The date in the first column then indicates when instruction in the skill began. When the pupil is tested a second time, put an *M* in the second column if mastery is achieved and record the date of mastery in the next column. Thus, anyone looking at the check list can tell whether the student mastered the skill before instruction or after instruction began, and when the skill was actually mastered.

Reading Skills Check List
FIRST LEVEL

On the following pages you will find the Reading Skills Check List: FIRST LEVEL. A group or individual recordkeeping form, "Class Record of Reading Skills: FIRST LEVEL," is also provided on pages 250–251.

Together, these forms offer a practical and optional individual and group record-keeping system for pinpointing students' reading progress. They provide a useful guide to instruction as well as a basis for conferences with other faculty, parents, and the student about the pupil's reading progress. These records can also be passed along to the next grade level teacher at the end of the year to provide evidence of where students are in the continuum of reading skills.

READING SKILLS CHECK LIST
FIRST LEVEL*

(Last Name)	(First Name)	(Name of School)
(Age)	(Grade Placement)	(Name of Teacher)

I. Vocabulary:
   A. Word Recognition
   1. Recognizes words with both upper- and lower-case letters at beginning
   2. Knows names of letters in sequence
   3. Is able to identify in various settings the following words usually found in pre-primers and primers:

___	a	___	eat	___	long	___	stop
___	about	___	farm	___	look	___	surprise
___	again	___	father	___	make	___	TV
___	all	___	fast	___	man	___	table
___	am	___	find	___	many	___	take
___	an	___	fine	___	may	___	thank
___	and	___	fish	___	me	___	that
___	apple	___	for	___	mitten	___	the
___	are	___	from	___	mother	___	their
___	as	___	fun	___	more	___	them
___	at	___	funny	___	morning	___	then
___	away	___	get	___	must	___	there
___	baby	___	girl	___	my	___	they
___	back	___	give	___	near	___	this
___	ball	___	go	___	new	___	tree
___	be	___	good	___	night	___	to
___	bed	___	good-by	___	no	___	too
___	been	___	green	___	not	___	toy
___	big	___	has	___	of	___	two
___	birthday	___	had	___	on	___	up
___	black	___	happy	___	one	___	us
___	blue	___	have	___	or	___	walk
___	boat	___	he	___	party	___	want
___	boy	___	help	___	pie	___	was
___	but	___	her	___	play	___	water
___	by	___	here	___	pretty	___	way
___	cake	___	hide	___	puppy	___	we
___	call	___	him	___	put	___	went
___	came	___	his	___	rabbit	___	were
___	can	___	home	___	ran	___	what
___	car	___	house	___	red	___	when
___	Christmas	___	how	___	ride	___	where
___	come	___	I	___	run	___	which
___	cookies	___	if	___	said	___	white
___	could	___	in	___	sat	___	who
___	cow	___	is	___	saw	___	will
___	cowboy	___	it	___	see	___	wish
___	daddy	___	jump	___	she	___	with
___	day	___	just	___	show	___	woman
___	did	___	kitten	___	sleep	___	work
___	dinner	___	know	___	so	___	would
___	dish	___	laugh	___	some	___	yellow
___	do	___	let	___	something	___	yes
___	dog	___	like	___	soon	___	you
___	down	___	little	___	splash	___	your

II. Word Analysis:

A. Sound-Symbol Associations
1. Associates consonant sounds to the following letters:

b	___	h	___	n	___	t	___
c (cat)	___	j	___	p	___	v	___
d	___	k	___	q	___	w	___
f	___	l	___	r	___	y	___
g (goat)	___	m	___	s	___	z	___

2. Names letters to represent consonant sounds heard in:
   a. initial position
   b. final position
   c. medial position
3. Discriminates between words using:
   a. initial letter cues
      (Which word is *hat? hat-foot*)
   b. final letter cues
      (Which word is *bear? bear-boat*)
4. Associates sounds to digraphs:

sh	___	th (*this* and *thin*)	___
wh	___	ch (*church*)	___

5. Associates sounds to two-letter blends:

st	___	fr	___	gr	___	sw	___
bl	___	fl	___	sp	___	br	___
pl	___	cl	___	sm	___	gr	___
tr	___	gl	___	sn	___	sl	___

6. Knows that the letters *a, e, i, o, u*, and combinations of these can represent several different sounds

B. Structural Analysis
1. Knows endings
   a. *ed* sound as "ed" in *wanted*
   b. *ed* sound as "d" in *moved*
   c. *ed* sound as "t" in *liked*
2. Recognizes compound words
   (*into, upon*)
3. Knows common word families

all	___	an	___	ell	___	ook	___	in	
at	___	ill	___	ay	___	ing	___	ish	
it	___	et	___	ake	___	ack	___	ight	

C. Word Form Clues
1. Recognizes upper- and lower-case letters
2. Recognizes words of different length
3. Recognizes words with double letters

III. Comprehension:

A. Understands that printed symbols represent objects or actions
B. Can follow printed directions
C. Can draw conclusions from given facts
D. Can recall from stories read aloud:
1. main idea
2. names of characters
3. important details
4. stated sequence
E. Can recall after silent reading:
1. main idea
2. names of characters
3. important details
4. stated sequence
F. Can distinguish between real and imaginary events
G. Uses context clues in word attack
H. Can suggest or select an appropriate title for a story
I. Can relate story content to own experiences

Vocabulary, Word Analysis & Comprehension Activities
FIRST LEVEL

The following activities will help you give students practice in the specific vocabulary, word analysis, and comprehension skills at the First Level. These materials provide for the following:

- Learning opportunities for specific reading skills
- Individual and group practice and/or enrichment
- Better understanding of the classwork
- Verification of skill mastery
- Corrective exercises in specific skills
- Homework activity directed to specific reading needs
- Practice for mastery
- Optimal use of teacher time

The exercises can be photocopied just as they appear for classroom use.
Complete answer keys for activities in this unit are provided on pages 241–248.

VOCABULARY   A. Word Recognition   1. *Upper- and lower-case letters at beginning*

DIRECTIONS: Cut out each word that begins with a lower-case letter on the right. Paste each word in the box by the same word that begins with an upper-case letter.

1. | Dog | | frog

2. | Hog | | dog

3. | Log | | log

4. | Frog | | hog

VOCABULARY   A. Word Recognition   1. *Upper- and lower-case letters at beginning*

DIRECTIONS: Draw a line from each word that begins with an upper-case letter to the same word that begins with a lower-case letter.

Part A.

1. Ping   Swing

2. ring   Ring

3. King   ding

4. Ding   king

5. swing   ping

_____

Part B.

6. look   took

7. Hook   Look

8. cook   Brook

9. Took   hook

10. brook   Cook

VOCABULARY   A. Word Recognition   1. *Upper- and lower-case letters at beginning*

DIRECTIONS: In each box, draw a line from the word that begins with an **upper-case** letter to the same word that begins with a lower-case letter.

1. it It at	5. bed Red red	9. noon Moon moon
2. pat Bat bat	6. dig Dig big	10. dump Jump jump
3. get Get pet	7. pen Pen ten	11. sick Kick kick
4. lip Lip sip	8. way Lay lay	12. sing Sing wing

VOCABULARY   A. Word Recognition   1. *Upper- and lower-case letters at beginning*

DIRECTIONS: Put an X on each box if the two words in it are not the same word.

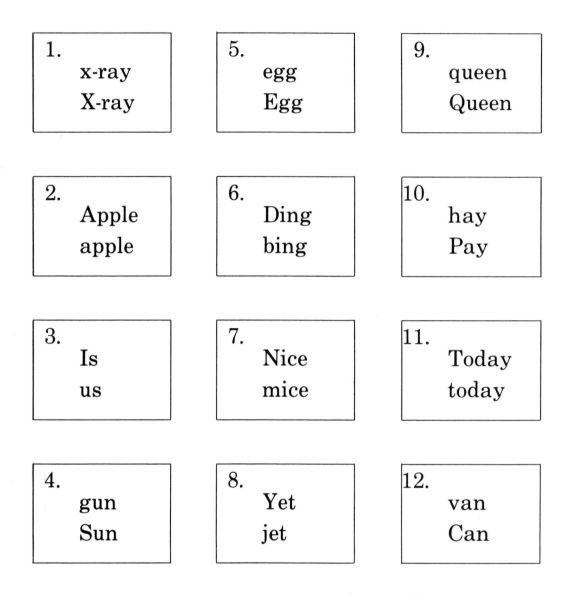

1.
x-ray
X-ray

5.
egg
Egg

9.
queen
Queen

2.
Apple
apple

6.
Ding
bing

10.
hay
Pay

3.
Is
us

7.
Nice
mice

11.
Today
today

4.
gun
Sun

8.
Yet
jet

12.
van
Can

VOCABULARY   **A. Word Recognition**   **1.** *Upper- and lower-case letters at beginning*

DIRECTIONS: In each box, draw a line between the lower-case and upper-case words that match.

1.			5.			9.		
		Wet			Dig			Joy
	yet	Jet		pig	Pig		joy	Toy
		Yet			Big			Boy
2.			**6.**			**10.**		
		Ray			Dot			Sit
	ray	Lay		got	Pot		sit	Kit
		Pay			Got			Fit
3.			**7.**			**11.**		
		Kid			Red			Hall
	lid	Lid		wed	Wed		tall	Fall
		Hid			Led			Tall
4.			**8.**			**12.**		
		How			Van			Dip
	how	Now		van	Can		zip	Zip
		Cow			Man			Rip

VOCABULARY   **A. Word Recognition**   **1. *Upper- and lower-case letters at beginning***

DIRECTIONS: Draw a line under the lower-case word that is the same as the upper-case first word in each row.

1. Jump	bump	jump	dump
2. Heat	heat	meat	neat
3. Coat	goat	boat	coat
4. Make	take	lake	make
5. Dear	dear	hear	near
6. Ride	wide	ride	hide
7. Bent	dent	tent	bent
8. Kind	find	wind	kind
9. Five	hive	five	live
10. Noon	noon	moon	soon

VOCABULARY   A. Word Recognition   2. *Names of letters in sequence*

DIRECTIONS: On each blank line, write the letter of the alphabet that comes after the letter that is given.

Part A.

1. A _____   4. E _____   7. J _____

2. C _____   5. H _____   8. X _____

3. M _____   6. O _____   9. W _____

DIRECTIONS: On each blank line, write the letter of the alphabet that comes before the letter that is given.

Part B.

10. _____ L   13. _____ Q   16. _____ Z

11. _____ V   14. _____ D   17. _____ I

12. _____ F   15. _____ S   18. _____ Y

VOCABULARY   A. Word Recognition   2. *Names of letters in sequence*

DIRECTIONS: On each blank line, write the letter that comes before or after the letter that is given.

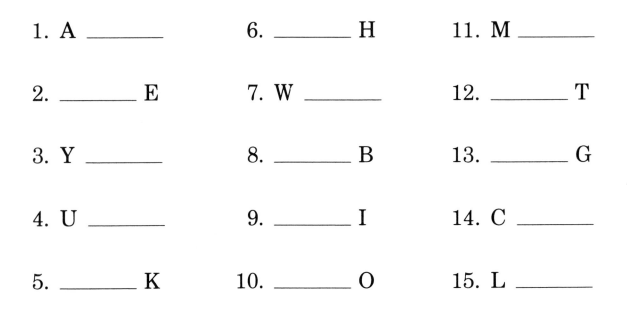

1. A _____   6. _____ H   11. M _____

2. _____ E   7. W _____   12. _____ T

3. Y _____   8. _____ B   13. _____ G

4. U _____   9. _____ I   14. C _____

5. _____ K   10. _____ O   15. L _____

VOCABULARY **A. Word Recognition** *2. Names of letters in sequence*

DIRECTIONS: On each blank line, write the letter that completes the three-letter sequence.

1. A B _____

2. _____ W X

3. D _____ F

4. T U _____

5. _____ R S

6. B _____ D

7. _____ I J

8. K _____ M

9. N O _____

10. _____V W

11. X Y _____

12. G H _____

13. _____ M N

14. P _____ R

VOCABULARY   A. Word Recognition   *2. Names of letters in sequence*

DIRECTIONS: Write the missing letters on the blank lines.

1. A B _____ D _____ F _____ H I _____ K _____

M N O _____ Q R _____ T U V _____ X Y _____

2. _____ B _____ _____ E _____ G _____ _____

J _____ L _____ _____ O P _____ _____ S

_____ U _____ W _____ _____ Z

VOCABULARY   A. Word Recognition   2. *Names of letters in sequence*

DIRECTIONS: Cut out the letters at the bottom of the page. Paste each one in its correct box so that the letters in each row will be in alphabetical order.

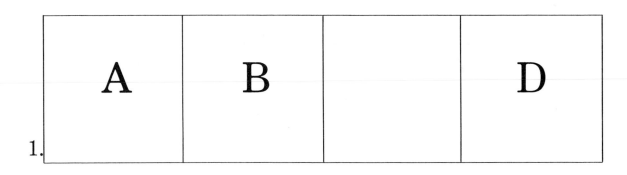

A	B		D

1.

L		N	O

2.

	U		W

3.

V	C	T	M

VOCABULARY   A. Word Recognition   2. *Names of letters in sequence*

DIRECTIONS: Cut out the letters at the bottom of the page. Paste each one in its correct box so that the letters in each row will be in alphabetical order.

W	X	Y	

1.

	H	I	

2.

P		R	S

3.

G	Z	J	Q

I

VOCABULARY   **A. Word Recognition**   **2. *Names of letters in sequence***

DIRECTIONS: Write the missing letters in the circles.

VOCABULARY   A. Word Recognition   3. *Words in preprimers and primers*

DIRECTIONS: In each box, draw a picture in the same color as the color word in the box.

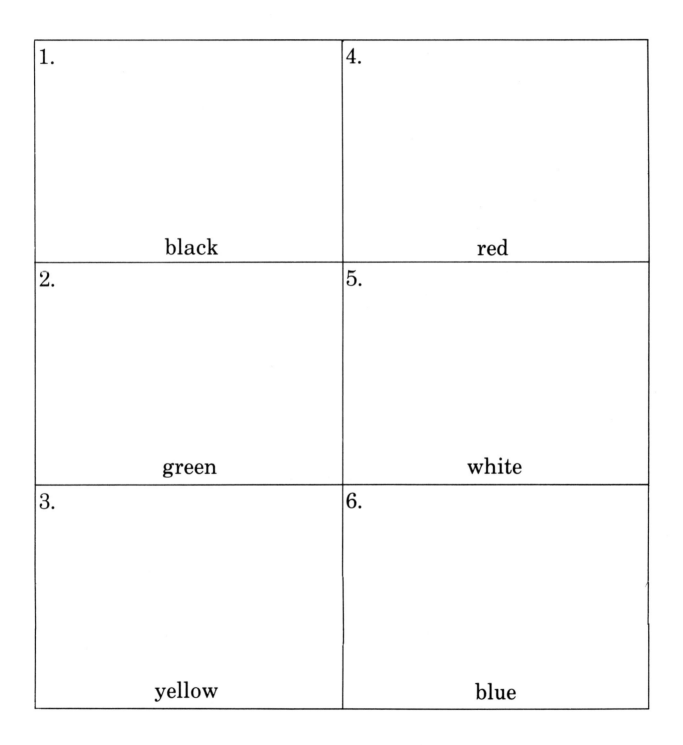

1.

black

4.

red

2.

green

5.

white

3.

yellow

6.

blue

VOCABULARY   A. Word Recognition   **3. *Words in preprimers and primers***

DIRECTIONS: In each box, draw a picture that shows something about the word in the box.

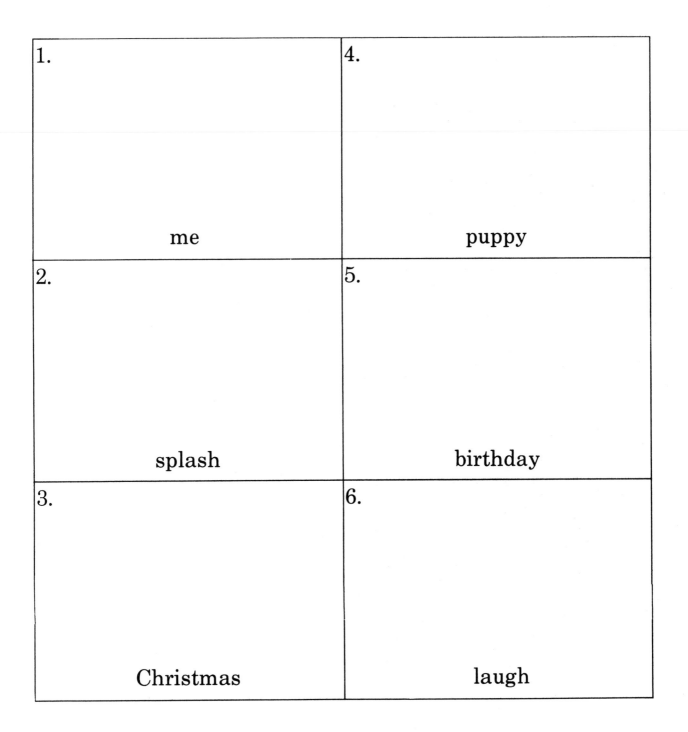

1. me	4. puppy
2. splash	5. birthday
3. Christmas	6. laugh

DIRECTIONS: In each box, draw a picture that shows something about the word in the box.

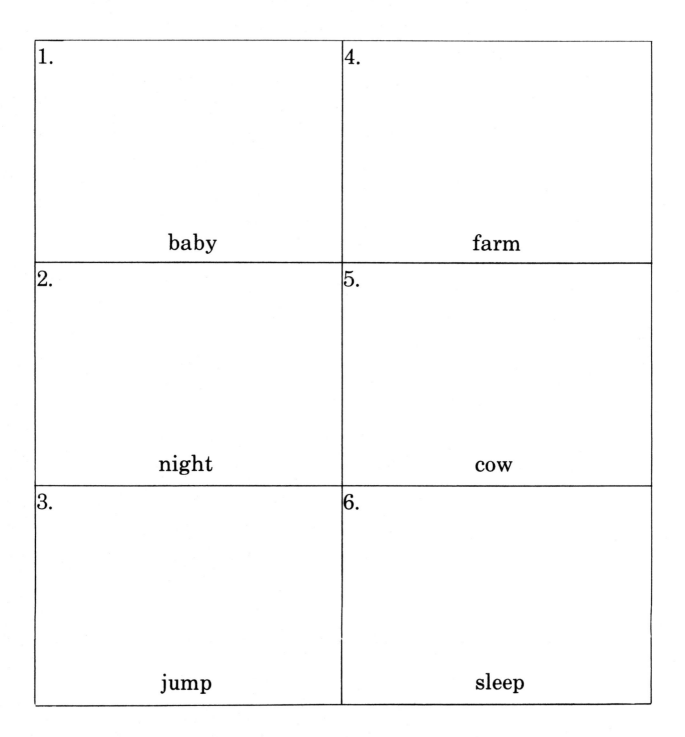

1. baby	4. farm
2. night	5. cow
3. jump	6. sleep

DIRECTIONS: Read the words below. In each box, write the word that names the picture in the box.

pie   table   cake   toy

1.	3.
_____	_____
2.	4.
_____	_____

VOCABULARY   **A. Word Recognition**   **3. *Words in preprimers and primers***

DIRECTIONS: Read the words below. In each box, write the word that names the picture in the box.

bed   kitten   girl   cookies

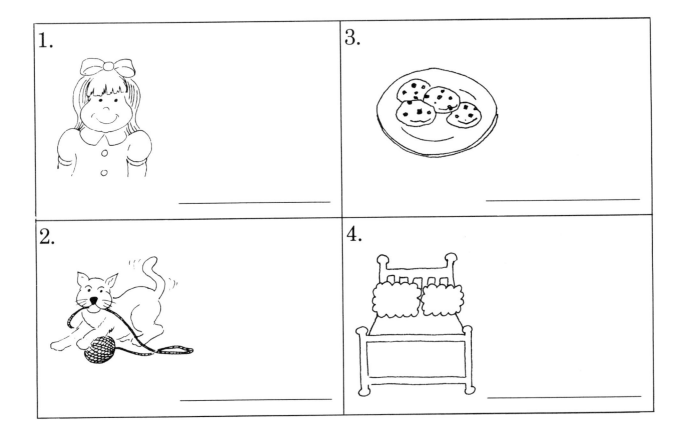

1. _____

2. _____

3. _____

4. _____

VOCABULARY   **A. Word Recognition**   **3. *Words in preprimers and primers***

DIRECTIONS: Draw a line from each picture to the word that names it.

1.

came

can

4.

been

boat

2.

two

too

5.

down

dish

3.

man

may

6.

tree

that

VOCABULARY   **A. Word Recognition**   *3. Words in preprimers and primers*

DIRECTIONS: Draw a line from each picture to the word that names it.

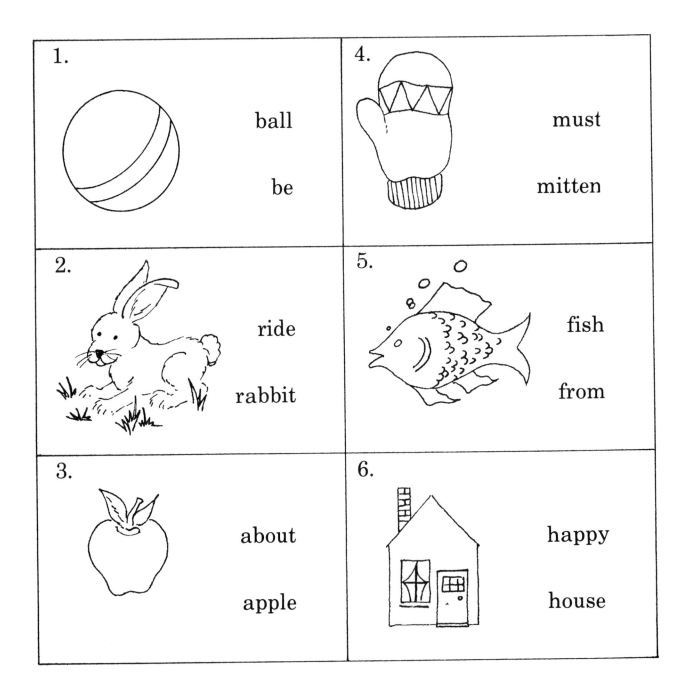

1.

ball

be

4.

must

mitten

2.

ride

rabbit

5.

fish

from

3.

about

apple

6.

happy

house

Name: _____ Date: _____

DIRECTIONS: Draw a line from each picture to the word that names it.

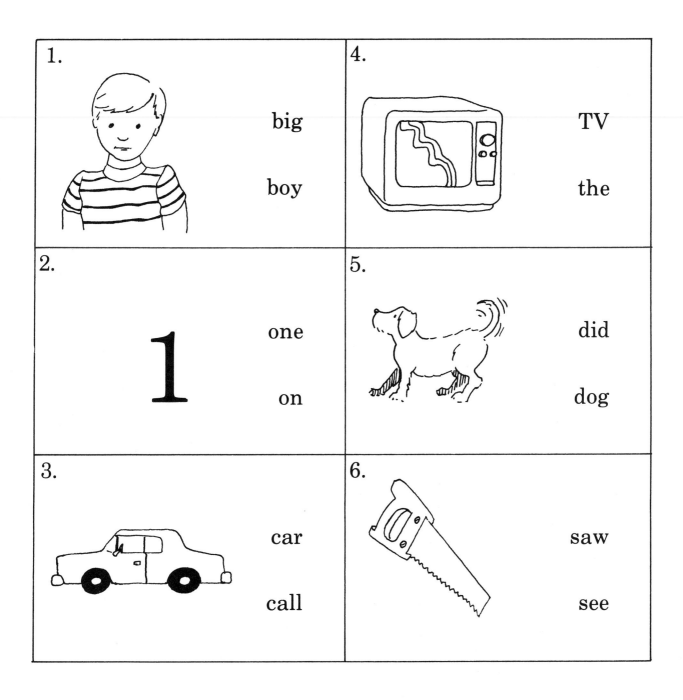

1. big boy	4. TV the
2. one on	5. did dog
3. car call	6. saw see

TEACHER DIRECTIONS: Use word pages 39–53 as practice sheets in classroom or home activities as you deem appropriate. Other options for the drill sheets are:

1. Word Bingo

   Number of players: Two to ten children can play. You or a child who can read all of the words can be the caller.

   Preparation: Run off two sheets for each word page you want to review. One of each of the two matching sheets will be a bingo board. Cut the words out of the remaining sheet to make word cards for the caller. Paste both the word sheets and word cards you want to review on oaktag (cards on 2″ × 2″ oaktag squares) and laminate them. Get enough markers so that each player will have 12. You may want to use dried beans, buttons, or bottle caps as markers.

   Directions: The caller reads one word at a time to the players. If they have the word on their bingo board, they cover it with a marker. The first player to correctly cover three words horizontally or four words vertically says "Bingo" and is the winner.

2. Go Fish

   Number of players: Two to six children can play.

   Preparation: Run off two sheets each for the word pages you want to review. Cut out the words, paste them on 2″ × 2″ oaktag squares, and laminate them.

   Directions: The dealer shuffles the cards and gives each player five cards. The extra cards are put in a stack at the center of the playing area.

   The first player calls on any child in the group to give him a word card to match one he has in his hand. If the child called has that card, he must give it to the player who asked for it. The pair is placed face up in front of the child who won it. If the first player asks another player for a card he does not have, he then draws from the deck of extra word cards. If the card he draws matches a word he has in his hand, he reads the word, places the pair in front of him, and draws again until he gets a word card that does not match one he has in his hand. The children may help each other read the words. The winner is the player with the greatest number of pairs after all of the cards have been matched.

3. Choose and Read

   Number of players: Two to six children can play. You or a child who can read all of the words can be the leader.

   Preparation: Run off the sheets with the words you want to review. Cut out the words, paste them on 2″ × 2″ oaktag squares, and laminate them.

   Directions: Lay all of the cards you want to review face down on a flat surface and mix them up. Each child takes a turn choosing a word card, turning it over, and reading it. If he reads the word correctly, he wins the card and gets to put it face up in front of him until the game is over. If he misses the word, he puts it back face down in the pile. The leader lets each player know if he read his word correctly or incorrectly. The winner is the player who has the greatest number of cards after all of the cards have been read.

VOCABULARY   A. Word Recognition   3. *Words in preprimers and primers*

TEACHER DIRECTIONS: Use the words in the learning activities as you deem appropriate. See the game activity suggestions on page 38.

a	about	again
all	am	an
and	apple	are
as	at	away

Name: _____ Date: _____

TEACHER DIRECTIONS: Use the words in the learning activities as you deem appropriate. See the game activity suggestions on page 38.

baby	back	ball
be	bed	been
big	birthday	black
blue	boat	boy

VOCABULARY   A. Word Recognition   3. *Words in preprimers and primers*

TEACHER DIRECTIONS: Use the words in the learning activities as you deem appropriate. See the game activity suggestions on page 38.

but	by	cake
call	came	can
car	Christmas	come
cookies	could	cow

I   41

VOCABULARY   A. Word Recognition   3. *Words in preprimers and primers*

TEACHER DIRECTIONS: Use the words in the learning activities as you deem appropriate. See the game activity suggestions on page 38.

cowboy	daddy	day
did	dinner	dish
do	dog	down
eat	farm	fast

VOCABULARY**A. Word Recognition****3. *Words in preprimers and primers***

TEACHER DIRECTIONS: Use the words in the learning activities as you deem appropriate. See the game activity suggestions on page 38.

father	find	fine
fish	for	from
fun	funny	get
girl	give	go

VOCABULARY   A. Word Recognition   3. *Words in preprimers and primers*

TEACHER DIRECTIONS: Use the words in the learning activities as you deem appropriate. See the game activity suggestions on page 38.

good	good-by	green
had	happy	has
have	he	help
her	here	hide

VOCABULARY   A. Word Recognition   3. *Words in preprimers and primers*

TEACHER DIRECTIONS: Use the words in the learning activities as you deem appropriate. See the game activity suggestions on page 38.

him	his	home
house	how	I
if	in	is
it	jump	just

VOCABULARY   **A. Word Recognition**   **3.** *Words in preprimers and primers*

TEACHER DIRECTIONS: Use the words in the learning activities as you deem appropriate. See the game activity suggestions on page 38.

kitten	know	laugh
let	like	little
long	look	make
man	many	may

VOCABULARY   A. Word Recognition   3. *Words in preprimers and primers*

TEACHER DIRECTIONS: Use the words in the learning activities as you deem appropriate. See the game activity suggestions on page 38.

me	mitten	more
morning	mother	must
my	near	new
night	no	not

TEACHER DIRECTIONS: Use the words in the learning activities as you deem appropriate. See the game activity suggestions on page 38.

of	on	one
or	party	pie
play	pretty	puppy
put	rabbit	ran

VOCABULARY   A. Word Recognition   3. *Words in preprimers and primers*

TEACHER DIRECTIONS: Use the words in the learning activities as you deem appropriate. See the game activity suggestions on page 38.

red	ride	run
said	sat	saw
see	she	show
sleep	so	some

VOCABULARY   **A. Word Recognition**   **3. *Words in preprimers and primers***

TEACHER DIRECTIONS: Use the words in the learning activities as you deem appropriate. See the game activity suggestions on page 38.

something	soon	splash
stop	surprise	table
take	thank	that
the	their	them

I

VOCABULARY   **A. Word Recognition**   **3. *Words in preprimers and primers***

TEACHER DIRECTIONS: Use the words in the learning activities as you deem appropriate. See the game activity suggestions on page 38.

then	there	they
this	to	too
toy	tree	TV
two	up	us

VOCABULARY   **A. Word Recognition**   3. *Words in preprimers and primers*

TEACHER DIRECTIONS: Use the words in the learning activities as you deem appropriate. See the game activity suggestions on page 38.

walk	want	was
water	way	we
went	were	what
when	where	which

VOCABULARY   A. Word Recognition   3. *Words in preprimers and primers*

TEACHER DIRECTIONS: Use the words in the learning activities as you deem appropriate. See the game activity suggestions on page 38.

white	who	will
wish	with	woman
work	would	yellow
yes	you	your

WORD ANALYSIS   **A. Sound-Symbol Associations**   1. *Consonant sounds:* b, c, d, f, g, m

DIRECTIONS: In each box, circle the words that begin with the same sound as the key letter.

b	boat love back hot	**c**	cane no say cold
d	dad dance do ball	**f**	flag blow fly parade
g	go pull goat push	**m**	me milk nose music

I

WORD ANALYSIS   A. Sound-Symbol Associations   1. *Consonant sounds:*
n, p, q, r, s, h

DIRECTIONS: In each box, circle the words that begin with the same sound as the key letter.

n	p
nut	pet
frog	rock
nail	gum
lace	pick

q	r
queen	rat
quiet	run
go	nut
push	rope

s	h
sand	hot
sun	kite
call	horse
apple	hug

DIRECTIONS: In each box, circle the words that begin with the same sound as the key letter.

h	horse hut lot fly	j	jacks just go glass
k	hit kite keg him	l	bet less love has
m	me no milk music	b	ball back house kite

WORD ANALYSIS   A. Sound-Symbol Associations   1. *Consonant sounds:*
t, v, w, x, y, z

DIRECTIONS: In each box, circle the words that begin with the same sound as the key letter.

t		v	
	toe		vote
	has		wheel
	tall		voice
	the		work
w		**x**	
	week		make
	vote		x-ray
	wet		now
	who		xylophone
y		**z**	
	you		zoo
	zest		you
	young		zebra
	go		yes

WORD ANALYSIS   A. Sound-Symbol Associations   1. *Consonant sound:* b

DIRECTIONS: Draw a line under each picture that begins with the same sound as the key letter.

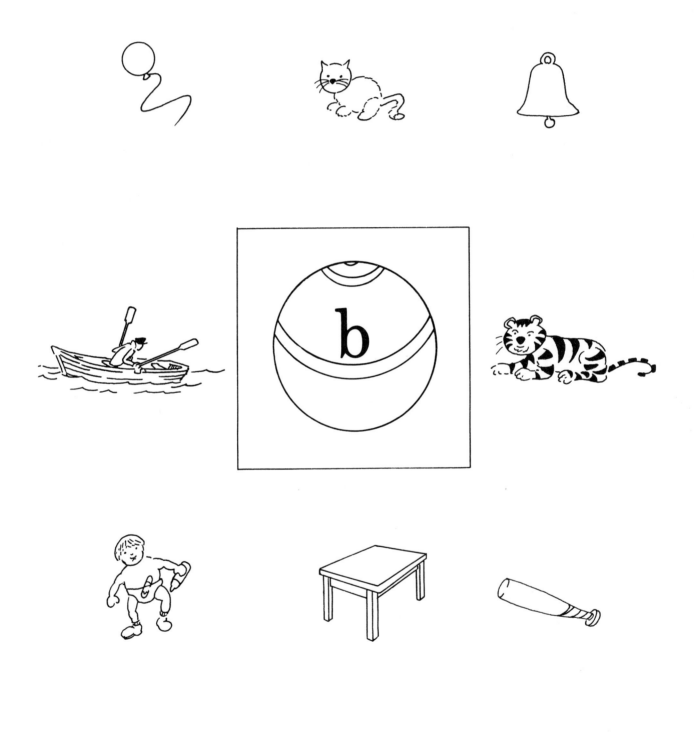

WORD ANALYSIS   **A. Sound-Symbol Associations**   **1. *Consonant sound:* c**

DIRECTIONS: Draw a circle around each picture that begins with the same sound as the key letter.

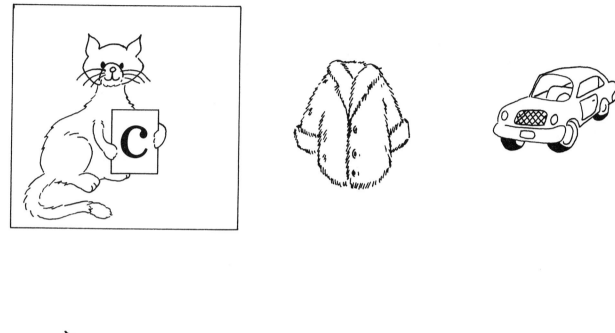

   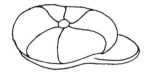

WORD ANALYSIS   A. Sound-Symbol Associations   1. *Consonant sound:* d

DIRECTIONS: Put an X through each picture that begins with the same sound as the key letter.

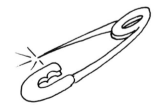

I

WORD ANALYSIS   A. Sound-Symbol Associations   1. *Consonant sound:* f

DIRECTIONS: Draw a line under each picture that begins with the same sound as the key letter.

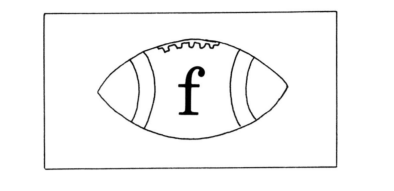

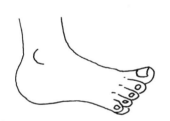

WORD ANALYSIS   **A. Sound-Symbol Associations**   1. *Consonant sound:* **g**

DIRECTIONS: Draw a line under each picture that begins with the same sound as the key letter.

I

WORD ANALYSIS   A. Sound-Symbol Associations   1. *Consonant sound:* h

DIRECTIONS: Draw a circle around each picture that begins with the same sound as the key letter.

Name: _____ Date: _____

WORD ANALYSIS   **A. Sound-Symbol Associations**   **1.** *Consonant sound:* j

---

DIRECTIONS: Put an X through each picture that begins with the same sound as the key letter.

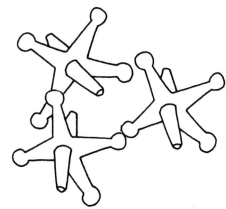

64   **I**

WORD ANALYSIS   **A. Sound-Symbol Associations**   1. *Consonant sound:* k

DIRECTIONS: Draw a line under each picture that begins with the same sound as the key letter.

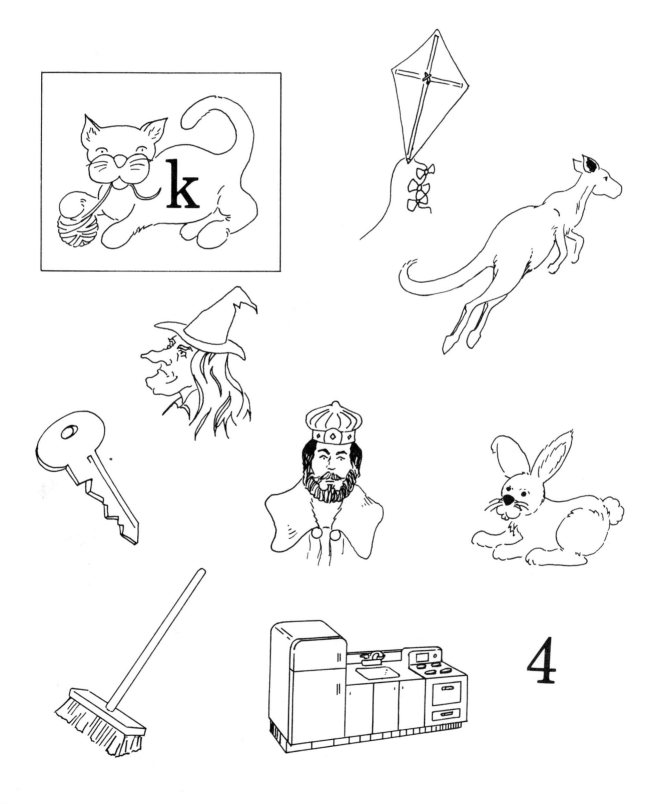

WORD ANALYSIS   A. Sound-Symbol Associations   1. *Consonant sound:* l

DIRECTIONS: Draw a circle around each picture that begins with the same sound as the key letter.

I

WORD ANALYSIS   **A. Sound-Symbol Associations**   **1. *Consonant sound:* m**

DIRECTIONS: Draw a circle around each picture that begins with the same sound as the key letter.

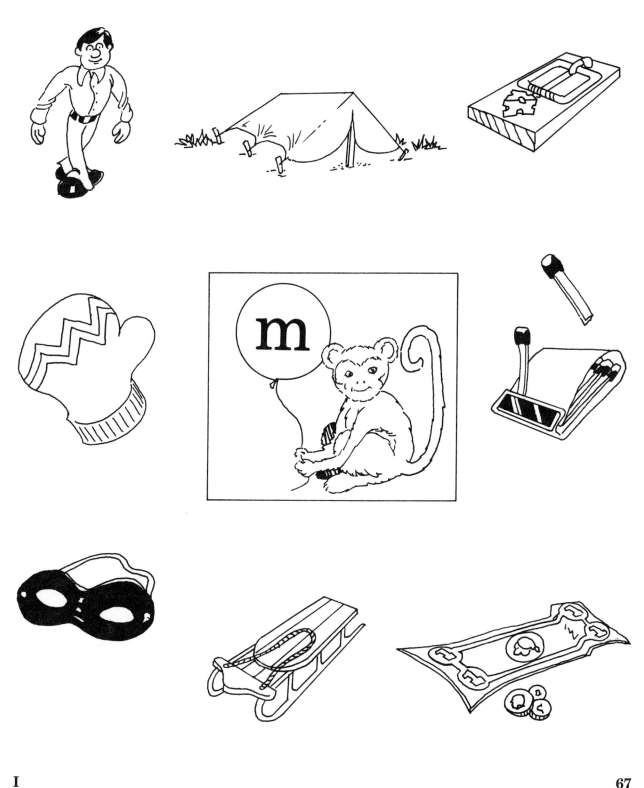

WORD ANALYSIS   **A. Sound-Symbol Associations**   **1.** *Consonant sound:* n

DIRECTIONS: Put an X through each picture that begins with the same sound as the key letter.

WORD ANALYSIS   **A. Sound-Symbol Associations**   1. *Consonant sound:* p

DIRECTIONS: Draw a line under each picture that begins with the same sound as the key letter.

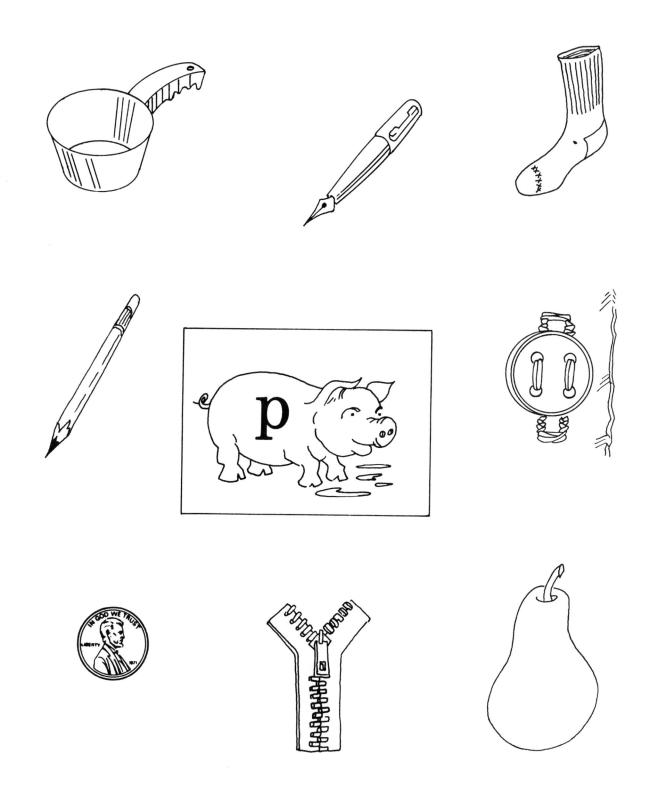

DIRECTIONS: Draw a circle around each picture that begins with the same sound as the key letter.

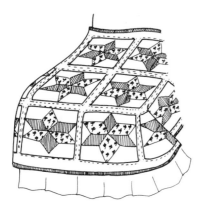

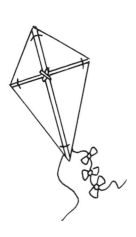

?

WORD ANALYSIS   A. Sound-Symbol Associations   1. *Consonant sound:* r

DIRECTIONS: Put an X through each picture that begins with the same sound as the key letter.

WORD ANALYSIS   A. Sound-Symbol Associations   1. *Consonant sound:* s

DIRECTIONS: Draw a line under each picture that begins with the same sound as the key letter.

I

WORD ANALYSIS   A. Sound-Symbol Associations   1. *Consonant sound:* t

DIRECTIONS: Draw a line under each picture that begins with the same sound as the key letter.

WORD ANALYSIS   **A. Sound-Symbol Associations**   **1. *Consonant sound:* v**

DIRECTIONS: Put an X through each picture that begins with the same sound as the key letter.

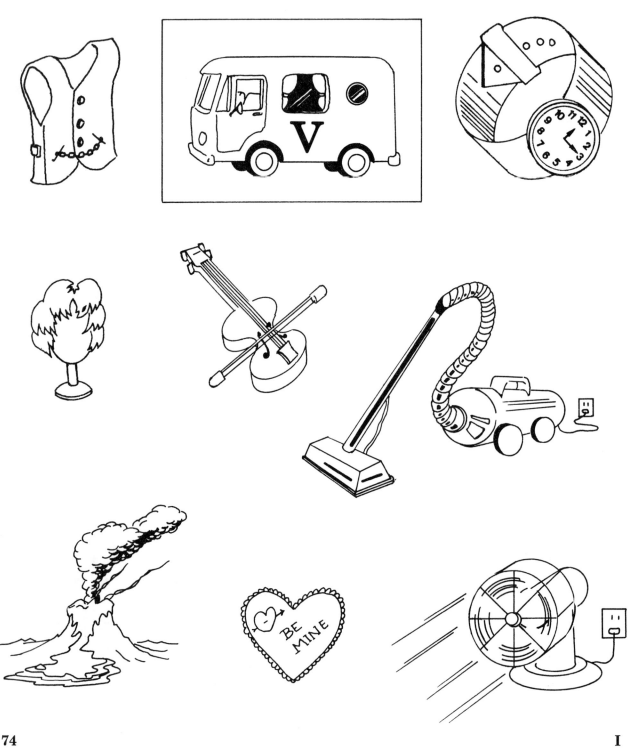

WORD ANALYSIS   A. Sound-Symbol Associations   1. *Consonant sound:* **w**

DIRECTIONS: Draw a circle around each picture that begins with the same sound as the key letter.

WORD ANALYSIS **A. Sound-Symbol Associations** **1.** *Consonant sound:* y

DIRECTIONS: Draw a circle around each picture that begins with the same sound as the key letter.

I

WORD ANALYSIS   A. Sound-Symbol Associations   1. *Consonant sound:* z

DIRECTIONS: Draw a line under each picture that begins with the same sound as the key letter

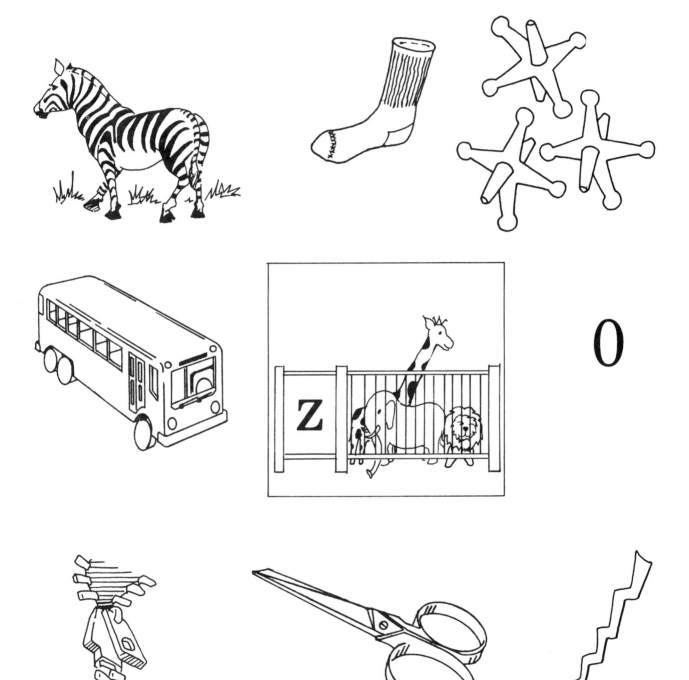

WORD ANALYSIS   A. Sound-Symbol Associations   1. *Consonant sounds:*
b, c, d, f, g

DIRECTIONS: Look at the word in the first box in each row. Draw a line under the words in the row that begin with the same consonant sound.

box	boat	man	ball
cup	sailor	cat	coat
down	dog	donut	pig
fog	fan	foot	hat
goose	nurse	gum	girl

1.
2.
3.
4.
5.

WORD ANALYSIS   A. Sound-Symbol Associations   1. *Consonant sounds:*
n, j, k, l, m

DIRECTIONS: Say the word in the first box in each row. Draw a line under the words in the row that begin with the same consonant sound.

1. hut	horse	helicopter	feather
2. jug	jet	jeep	yo-yo
3. keep	zebra	king	key
4. little	ladder	lock	rat
5. money	money	moon	nail

WORD ANALYSIS   A. Sound-Symbol Associations   1. *Consonant sounds:*
                                                        n, p, q, r, s

DIRECTIONS: Say the word in the first box in each row. Draw a circle around the words in the row that begin with the same consonant sound.

new	net	turkey	nine
puppy	yarn	pie	pumpkin
queen	queen	question	watermelon
run	ring	rake	wheel
show	volcano	sailor	six

1.
2.
3.
4.
5.

I

WORD ANALYSIS   A. Sound-Symbol Associations   1. *Consonant sounds:*
t, v, w, y, z

DIRECTIONS: Say the word in the first box in each row. Draw a circle around the words in the row that begin with the same consonant sound.

table	ten	girl	tiger
vote	fire	vest	violin
wish	watch	witch	house
yellow	yawn	star	yo-yo
zoo	zebra	sock	zipper

1.
2.
3.
4.
5.

DIRECTIONS: Draw a line from each letter to the picture that begins with the same sound.

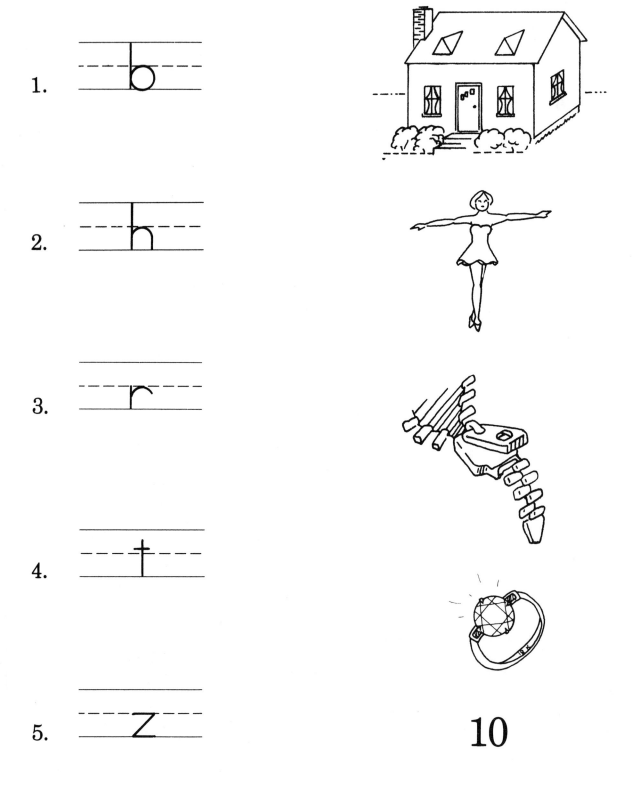

1. b

2. h

3. r

4. t

5. z

10

Name: _____ Date: _____

DIRECTIONS: Draw a line from each letter to the picture that begins with the same sound.

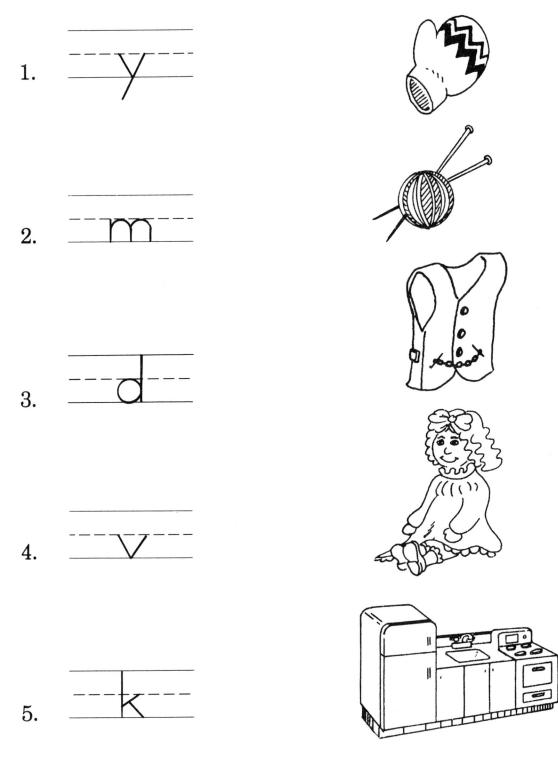

1. y

2. m

3. d

4. v

5. k

WORD ANALYSIS   **A. Sound-Symbol Associations**   **2. *Consonant sounds:***
    a. Initial position

DIRECTIONS: Draw a line from each letter to the picture that begins with the same sound.

1. C

2. J

3. n

4. S

5. W

WORD ANALYSIS   A. Sound-Symbol Associations   2. *Consonant sounds:*
                                                      a. Initial position

DIRECTIONS: Draw a line from each letter to the picture that begins with the same sound.

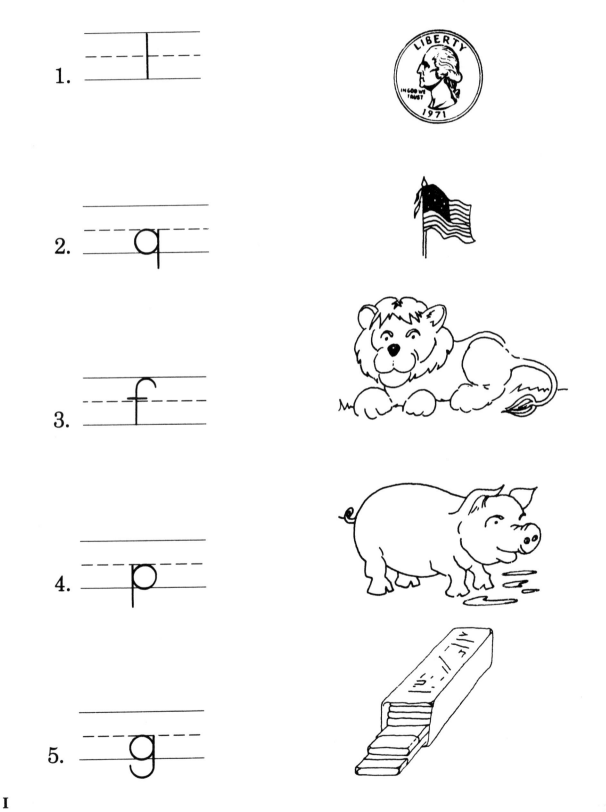

1.

2. q

3. f

4. p

5. g

WORD ANALYSIS **A. Sound-Symbol Associations** **2. *Consonant sounds:***
a. Initial position

DIRECTIONS: Say the words for the pictures in each row. In the blank, write the letter for the beginning sound you hear.

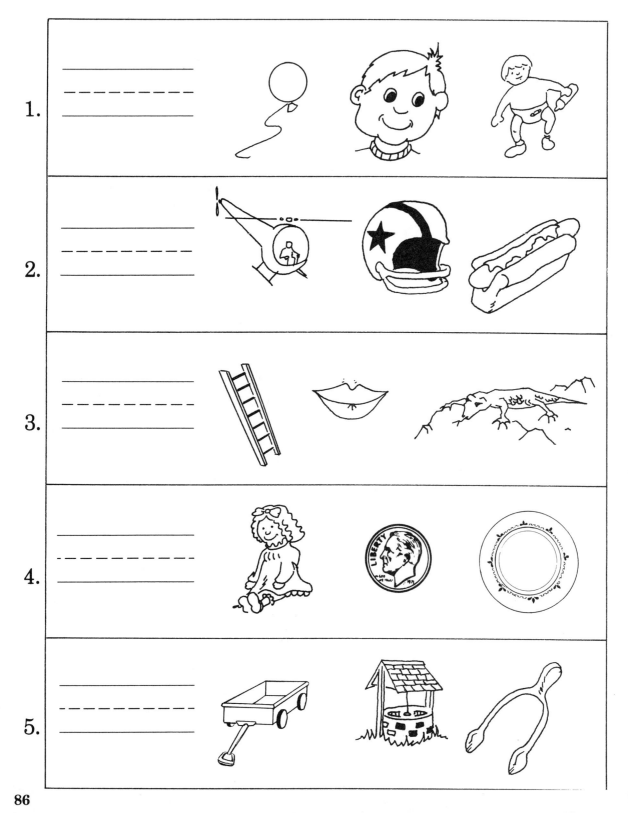

I

WORD ANALYSIS   A. Sound-Symbol Associations   2. *Consonant sounds:*
  a. Initial position

DIRECTIONS: Say the word for each picture. In the blank, write the letter for the beginning sound.

WORD ANALYSIS   **A. Sound-Symbol Associations**   **2. *Consonant sounds:***
b. Final position

DIRECTIONS: In each row, draw a line under the picture that ends with the same sound as the key letter.

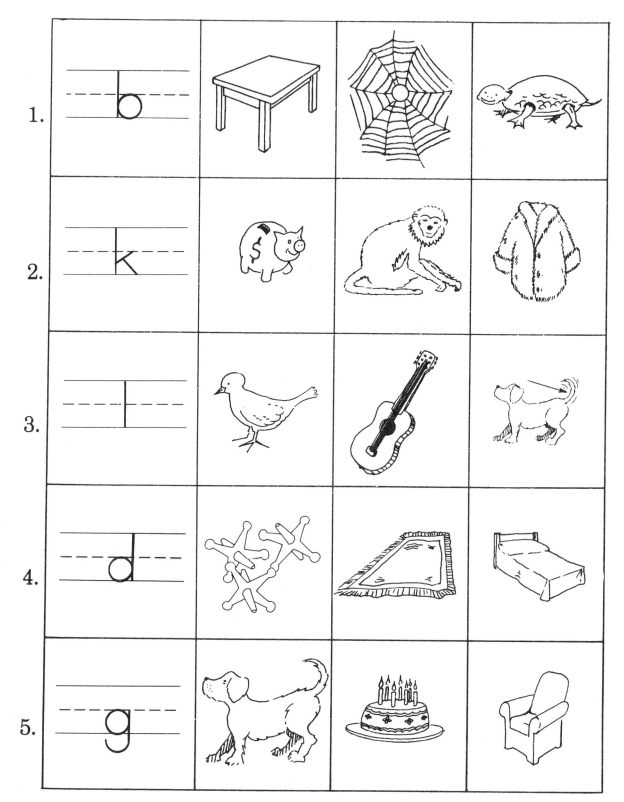

Name: _____ Date: _____

WORD ANALYSIS   A. Sound-Symbol Associations   2. *Consonant sounds:*
                                                    b. Final position

DIRECTIONS: In each row, draw a line under the picture that ends with the same sound as the key letter.

I   89

DIRECTIONS: Draw a line from each letter to the picture that ends with the same sound.

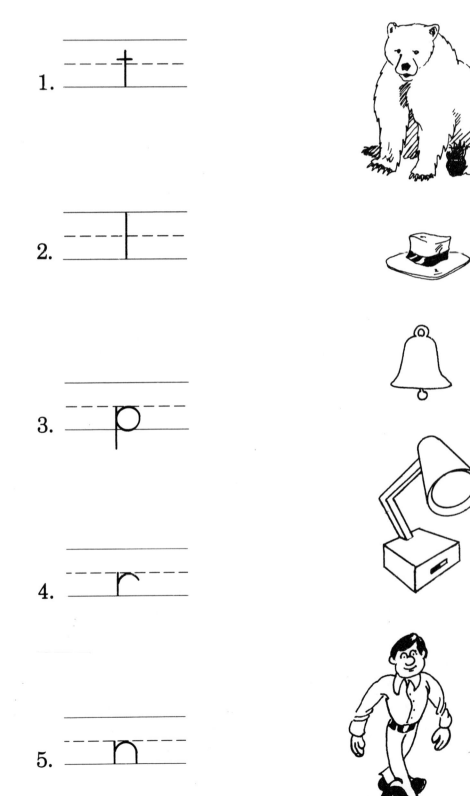

1. t

2. t

3. p

4. r

5. n

Name: _____ Date: _____

DIRECTIONS: Say the word for each picture. In the blank, write the letter that makes the last sound you hear.

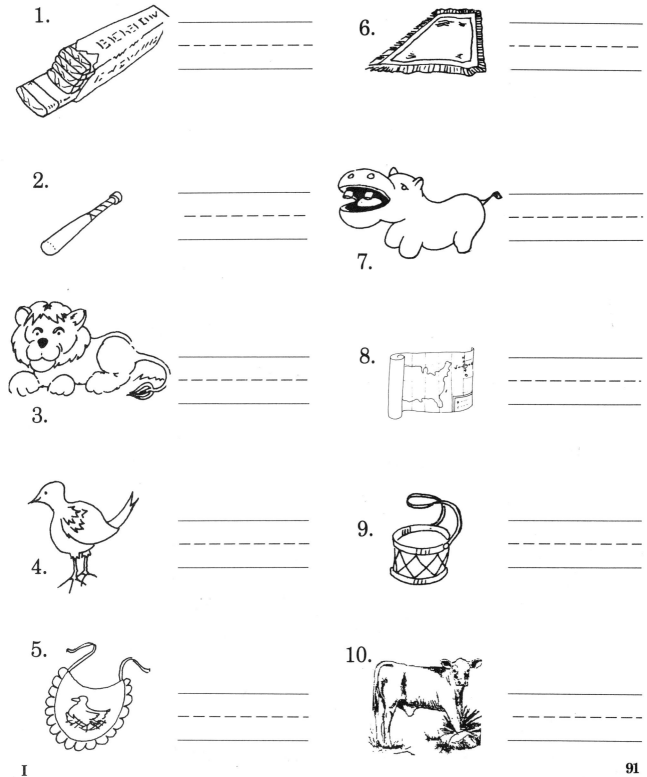

1. _____

6. _____

2. _____

7. _____

3. _____

8. _____

4. _____

9. _____

5. _____

10. _____

WORD ANALYSIS   A. Sound-Symbol Associations   2. *Consonant sounds:*
b. Final position

DIRECTIONS: Draw a line under the word that names each picture.

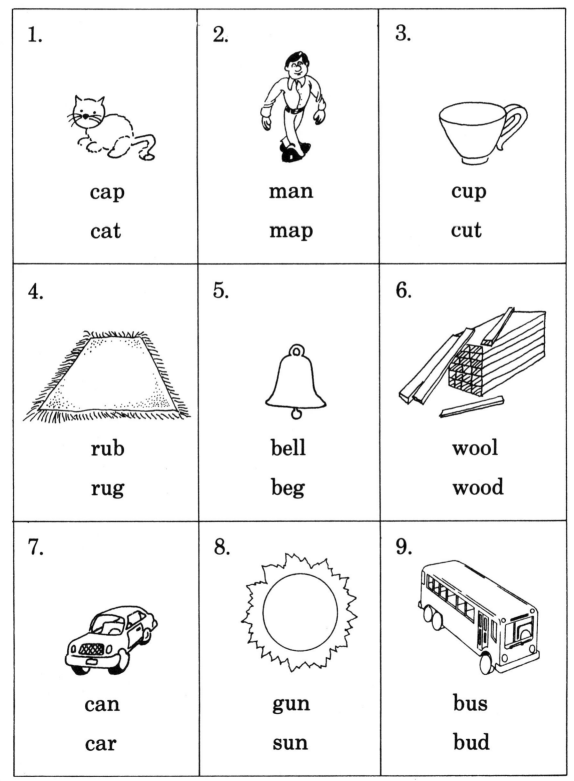

1.	2.	3.
cap	man	cup
cat	map	cut
4.	5.	6.
rub	bell	wool
rug	beg	wood
7.	8.	9.
can	gun	bus
car	sun	bud

WORD ANALYSIS   A. **Sound-Symbol Associations**   2. *Consonant sounds:*
c. Medial position

DIRECTIONS: In each row, draw a line under the picture that has the same middle sound as the key letter.

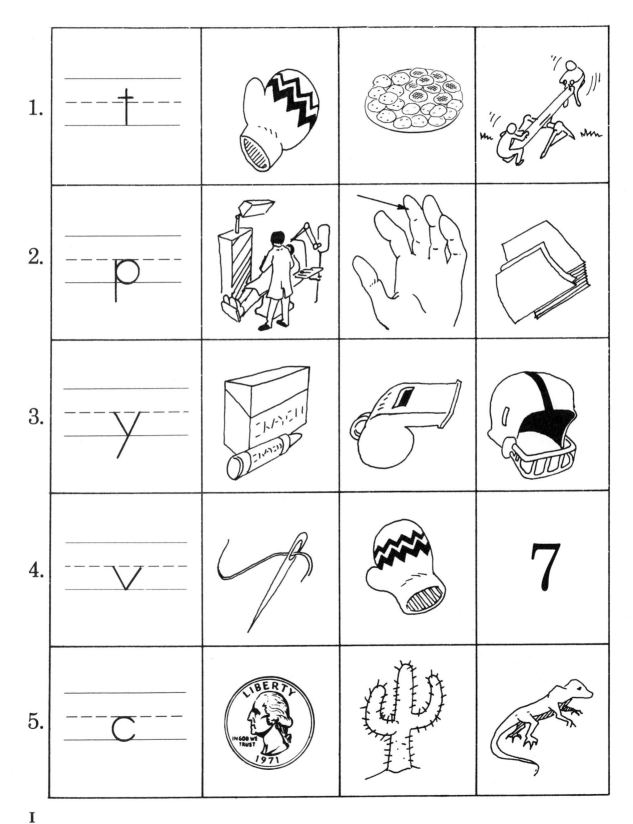

WORD ANALYSIS   A. Sound-Symbol Associations   2. *Consonant sounds:*
c. Medial position

DIRECTIONS: In each row, draw a line under the picture that has the same middle sound as the key letter.

WORD ANALYSIS   A. Sound-Symbol Associations   2. *Consonant sounds:*
c. Medial position

DIRECTIONS: Say the word for each picture. In the blank, write the missing letter for the sound you hear in the middle of each word.

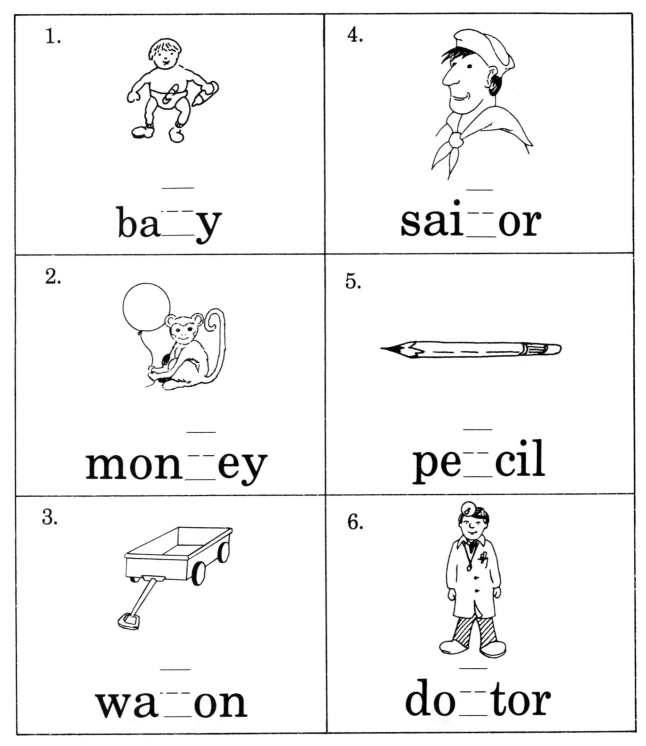

1. ba_y

2. mon_ey

3. wa_on

4. sai_or

5. pe_cil

6. do_tor

WORD ANALYSIS   A. Sound-Symbol Associations   2. *Consonant sounds:*
c. Medial position

DIRECTIONS: Say the word for each picture. In the blank, write the missing letter for the sound you hear in the middle of each word.

1.

wa__er

4.

lea__es

2.

bee__ive

5.

pa__er

3.

so__a

6.

wo__an

WORD ANALYSIS A. Sound-Symbol Associations 3. *Discriminates between words*
                                                  a. Initial letter cues

DIRECTIONS: Cut out the words. Paste each word in the box next to the picture for the word.

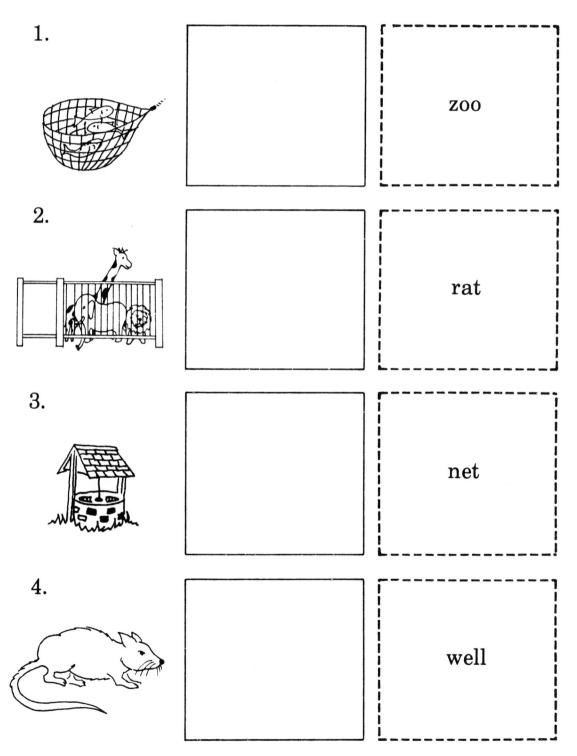

1.

zoo

2.

rat

3.

net

4.

well

WORD ANALYSIS A. Sound-Symbol Associations 3. *Discriminates between words*
                                             a. Initial letter cues

DIRECTIONS: Put an X through the picture of the word in each row.

WORD ANALYSIS A. Sound-Symbol Associations 3. *Discriminates between words*
a. Initial letter cues

DIRECTIONS: In each row, draw a line under the word that names the key picture.

1.	kitten	mitten
2.	bee	tree
3.	hat	cat
4.	pail	nail
5.	tent	sent

WORD ANALYSIS **A. Sound-Symbol Associations 3.** *Discriminates between words*
                                         a. Initial letter cues

DIRECTIONS: In each box, draw a line from the key word to the picture.

1. cat	6. king
2. jet	7. lock
3. soap	8. house
4. yarn	9. goat
5. pen 10	10. fire

WORD ANALYSIS A. Sound-Symbol Associations 3. *Discriminates between words*
b. Final letter cues

DIRECTIONS: Cut out the words. Paste each word in the box next to the picture it names.

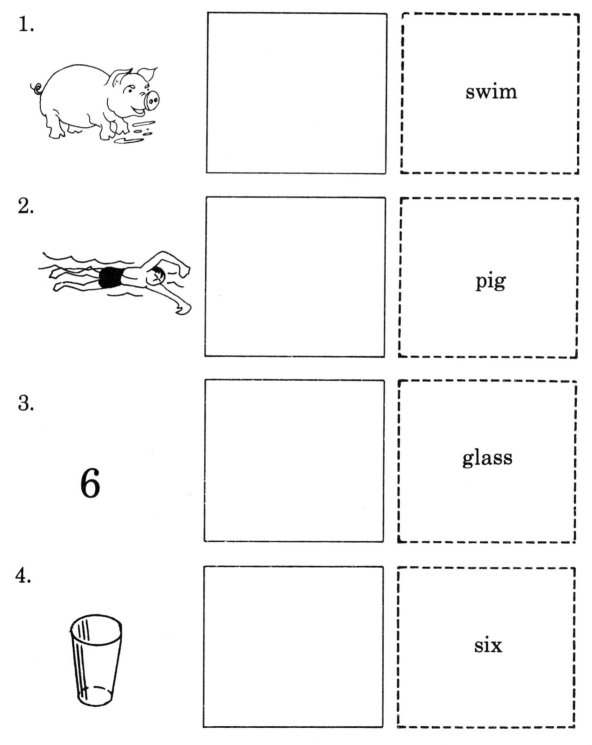

1.

swim

2.

pig

3.

6

glass

4.

six

Name: _____   Date: _____

WORD ANALYSIS A. Sound-Symbol Associations 3. *Discriminates between words*
b. Final letter cues

DIRECTIONS: In each row, draw a line under the picture that names the key word.

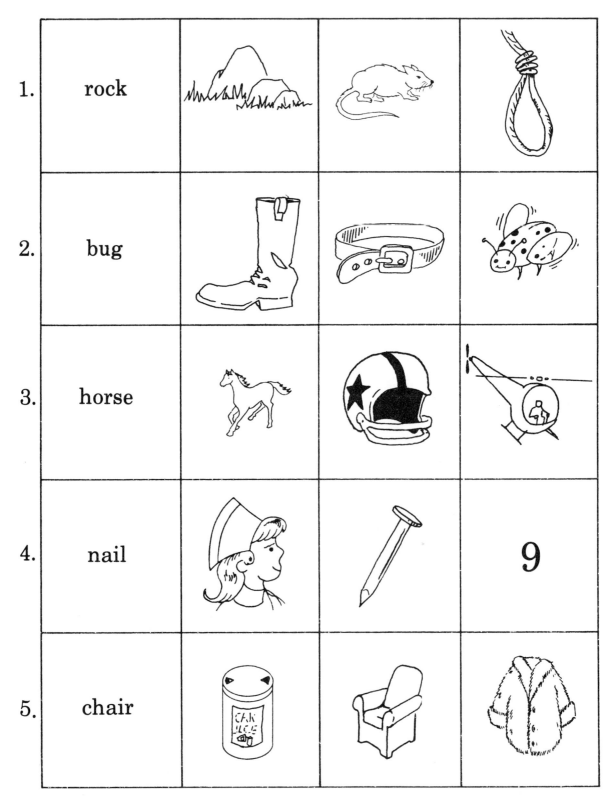

WORD ANALYSIS A. Sound-Symbol Associations 3. *Discriminates between words*
b. Final letter cues

DIRECTIONS: In each row, draw a line under the word that names the key picture.

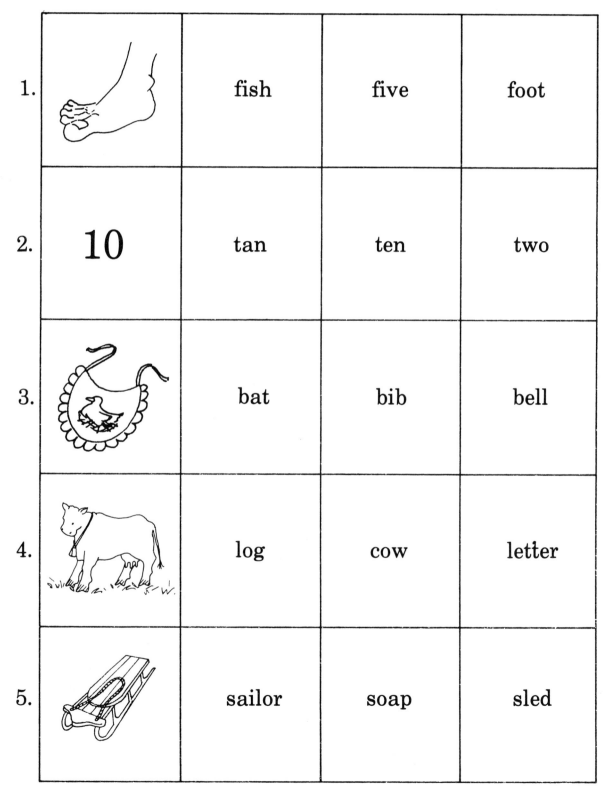

1.	fish	five	foot
2.	tan	ten	two
3.	bat	bib	bell
4.	log	cow	letter
5.	sailor	soap	sled

I

WORD ANALYSIS **A. Sound-Symbol Associations 3. *Discriminates between words***
                                      b. Final letter cues

DIRECTIONS: **Match the word with the picture.**

1. flag	6. bird
2. drum	7. map
3. coat	8. fox
4. girl	9. jet
5. van	10. bus

WORD ANALYSIS   **A. Sound-Symbol Associations**   **4.** *Digraph:* sh

DIRECTIONS: Put an X through the pictures that begin with the **sh** sound.

Name: _____ Date: _____

WORD ANALYSIS   A. Sound-Symbol Associations   4. *Digraph:* wh

DIRECTIONS: Draw a circle around each picture that begins with the **wh** sound.

106   I

WORD ANALYSIS   A. Sound-Symbol Associations   4. *Digraph:* th

DIRECTIONS: Draw a line under the pictures that begin with the **th** sound.

WORD ANALYSIS   A. Sound-Symbol Associations   4. *Digraph:* ch

DIRECTIONS: Put an X through the pictures for the words that begin with the **ch** sound.

I

Name: _____   Date: _____

DIRECTIONS: Say the word for the picture in each box. Write the letters of the beginning digraph sound.

WORD ANALYSIS   A. Sound-Symbol Associations   5. *Blends:* st, bl, pl

DIRECTIONS: Say the word for the picture in each box. Write.the letters that make the beginning blend sound.

st

bl

pl

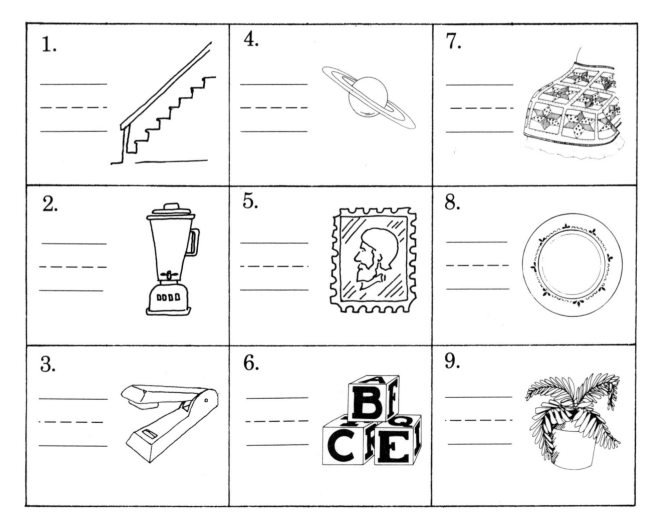

1. _____	4. _____	7. _____
2. _____	5. _____	8. _____
3. _____	6. _____	9. _____

WORD ANALYSIS   **A. Sound-Symbol Associations**   **5.** *Blends:* tr, fr

DIRECTIONS: Draw a circle around each picture that begins with the **tr** sound.

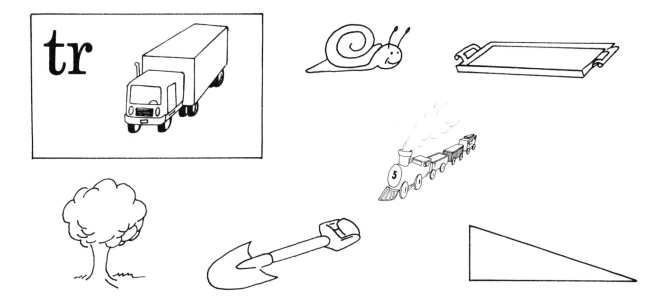

DIRECTIONS: Draw a circle around each picture that begins with the **fr** sound.

WORD ANALYSIS   A. Sound-Symbol Associations   5. *Blends:* fl, gl, cl

DIRECTIONS: Say the word for the picture in each box. Write the letters of the beginning sound.

I

WORD ANALYSIS   **A. Sound-Symbol Associations**   **5.** *Blends:* **gr, sp**

DIRECTIONS: Put an X through each picture that begins with the same sound as the key picture.

WORD ANALYSIS   **A. Sound-Symbol Associations**   5. *Blends:* sm, sn, sw

DIRECTIONS: Draw a line from the key picture in each box to the pictures that begin with the same sound.

WORD ANALYSIS   A. Sound-Symbol Associations   5. *Blends:* br, gr, sl, st, bl, pl

DIRECTIONS: In each row, circle the words that begin with the same consonant blend as the first word.

1. broom   bread   clear   shell   bridge

2. grasshopper   chin   please   grow   grape

3. slip   slide   ship   sled   shelf

4. stick   slow   stop   shop   star

5. blow   blink   flow   block   flip

6. please   plate   glow   chain   pliers

7. brush   brick   bring   plane   grip

8. green   garden   grade   gone   grape

9. sled   slap   sleep   skate   stool

10. stove   step   stack   skate   skunk

DIRECTIONS: In the space provided, write the consonant blend that you hear at the beginning of each word.

st	bl	pl

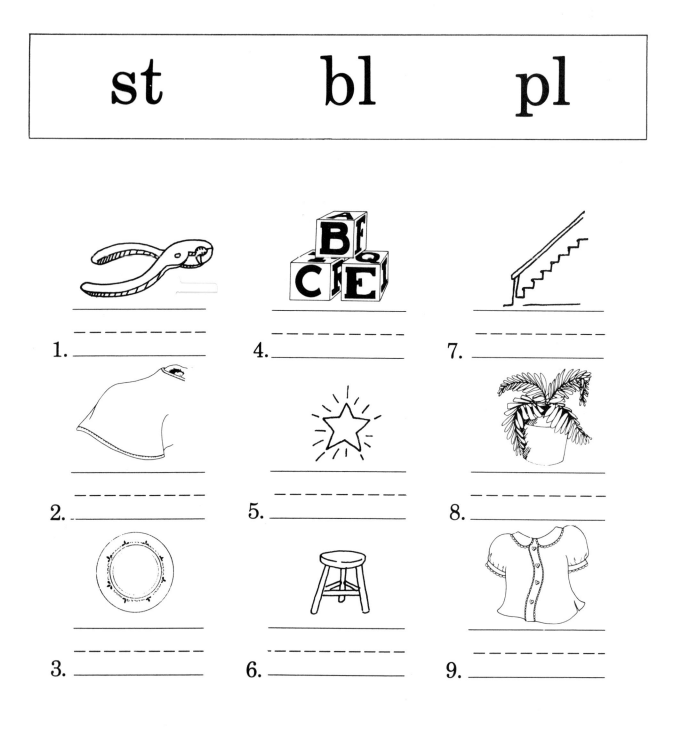

1. _____

2. _____

3. _____

4. _____

5. _____

6. _____

7. _____

8. _____

9. _____

WORD ANALYSIS   **A. Sound-Symbol Associations**   **5.** *Blends:* **tr, fr, fl, cl, gl**

DIRECTIONS: When you say the name of the picture, you hear a consonant blend. Draw a line from the consonant blend to each picture that begins with the same sound.

1. **tr**

2. **fr**

3. **fl**

4. **cl**

5. **gl**

Name: _____   Date: _____

DIRECTIONS: When you say the name of the picture, you hear a consonant blend. Under the picture, write the consonant blend that you hear.

gr	sp	sm

1.

- - - - - - - - -

2.

- - - - - - - - -

3.

- - - - - - - - -

4.

- - - - - - - - -

5.

- - - - - - - - -

6.

- - - - - - - - -

7.

- - - - - - - - -

8.

- - - - - - - - -

9.

- - - - - - - - -

I

WORD ANALYSIS   **A. Sound-Symbol Associations**   **5.** *Blends:* sn, sw, br, gr, sl

DIRECTIONS: Listen as you say the consonant blend sounds in the middle column. Draw a line from the consonant blend to the pictures that begin with the same sound.

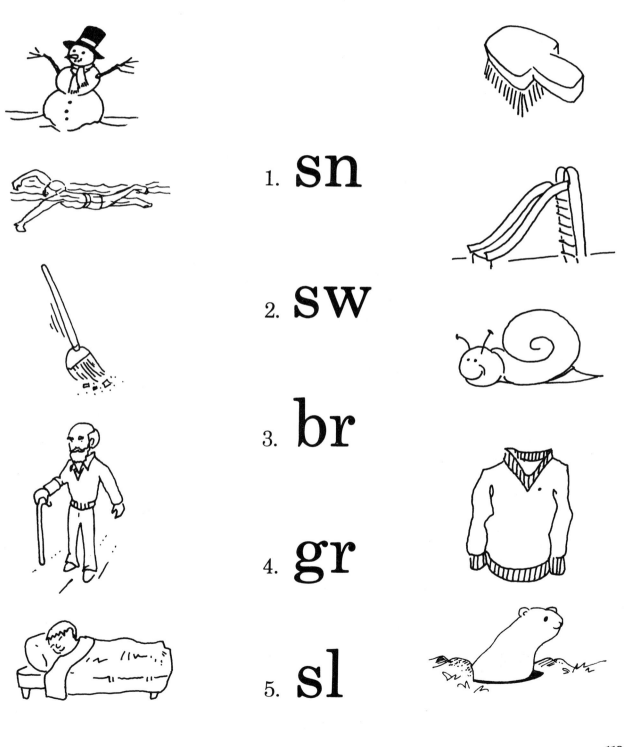

1. **sn**

2. **sw**

3. **br**

4. **gr**

5. **sl**

I

WORD ANALYSIS   A. Sound-Symbol Associations   6. *Vowel:* a

DIRECTIONS: Say the name of the picture in each box. Draw a circle around each picture that has a short **a** vowel sound like in **cat**. Put an X through each picture that has a long **a** vowel sound like in **rake**.

WORD ANALYSIS   **A. Sound-Symbol Associations**   **6. _Vowel:_ e**

DIRECTIONS: Say the name of the picture in each box. Draw a circle around each picture that has a short **e** vowel sound like in **bed**. Put an X through each picture that has a long **e** vowel sound like in **feet**.

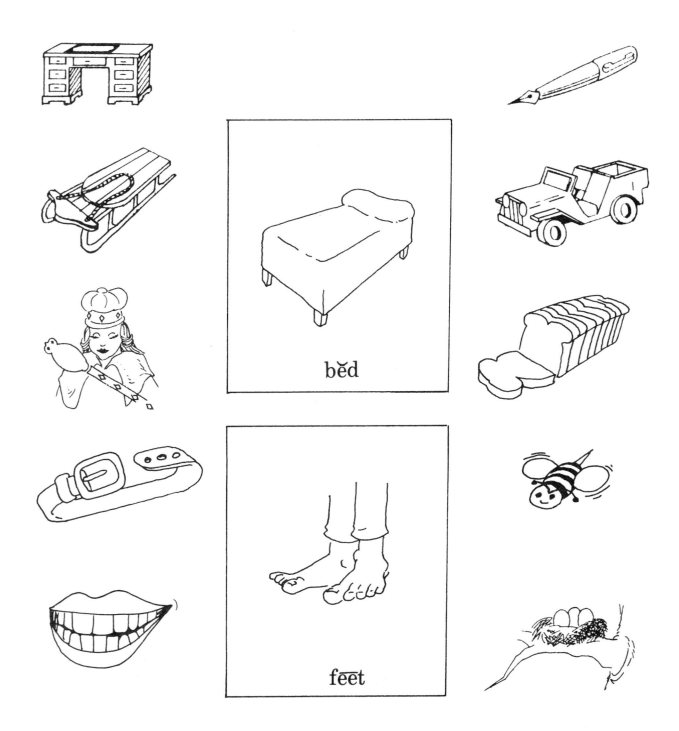

běd

fēet

WORD ANALYSIS   **A. Sound-Symbol Associations**   **6.** *Vowel:* i

DIRECTIONS: Say the name of the picture in each box. Draw a circle around each picture that has a short **i** vowel sound like in **bib**. Put an X through each picture that has a long **i** sound like in **bike**.

       I

DIRECTIONS: Read each word. Write the words that have a short **o** vowel sound, like in **top**, in column A. Write the words that have a long **o** vowel sound, like in **boat**, in column B.

mop	toe	rose
soap	bone	box
rock	dog	blocks
note	goat	dock

Column A	Column B
top	**boat**

_____   _____

_____   _____

_____   _____

_____   _____

_____   _____

_____   _____

DIRECTIONS: Say the name of the picture in each box. Draw a circle around each picture that has a short **u** vowel sound like in **cup**. Put an X through each picture that a long **u** vowel sound like in **mule**.

WORD ANALYSIS   A. Sound-Symbol Associations   6. *Vowels:* a, e, i, o, u

DIRECTIONS: Say the word in each box. Circle the vowel you hear in the word.

1.

a e i o u

2.

a e i o u

3.

a e i o u

4.

a e i o u

5.

a e i o u

6.

a e i o u

7.

a e i o u

8.

a e i o u

9.

a e i o u

10.

a e i o u

11.

a e i o u

12.

a e i o u

Name: _____   Date: _____

DIRECTIONS: Say the name of each picture. Write the letter that makes the long vowel sound.

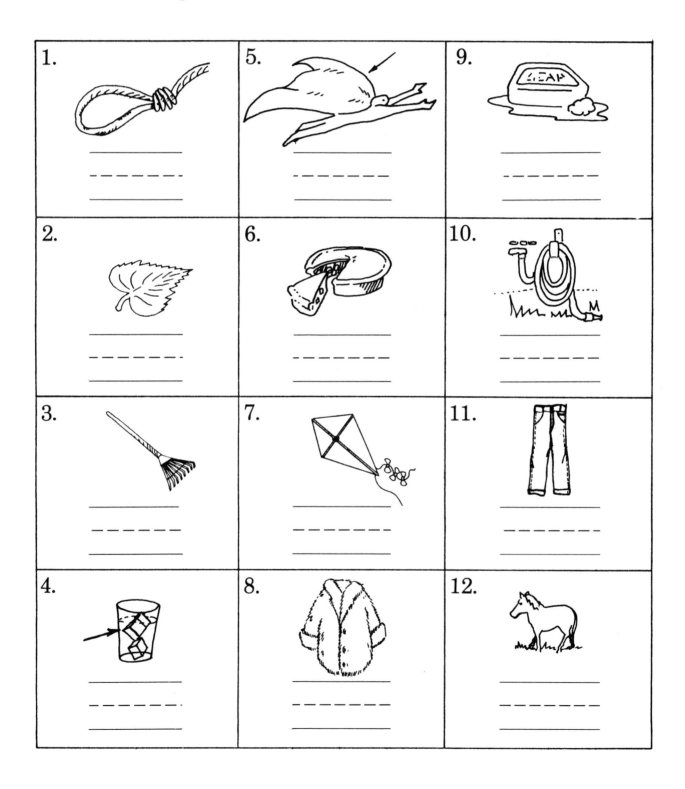

WORD ANALYSIS **B. Structural Analysis** **1. *Endings***
 a. *ed* sound as "ed"

DIRECTIONS: Trace over the words that end with the same **ed** sound as the key word.

pasted

1.

6.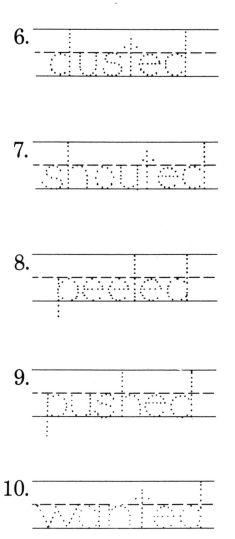

2.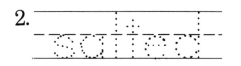

7.

3.

8.

4.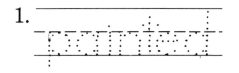

9.

5.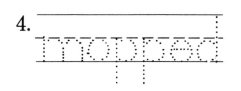

10.

WORD ANALYSIS   B. Structural Analysis   1. *Endings*
                                          a. *ed* sound as "ed"

DIRECTIONS: In each sentence, circle the word that ends with an **ed** sound. Write the word under the sentence.

1. Mary wanted the cake.
         baked

_____
- - - - - - - - - - - - -
_____

2. Dad washed the car.
        started

_____
- - - - - - - - - - - - -
_____

3. John climbed the tree.
         planted

_____
- - - - - - - - - - - - -
_____

4. She needed the coat.
        dropped

_____
- - - - - - - - - - - - -
_____

5. The children skated.
                 played.

_____
- - - - - - - - - - - - -
_____

6. Mother salted the meat.
           cooked

_____
- - - - - - - - - - - - -
_____

7. Sue colored the picture.
        painted

_____
- - - - - - - - - - - - -
_____

8. Fred shouted at the dog.
         laughed

_____
- - - - - - - - - - - - -
_____

WORD ANALYSIS   B. Structural Analysis   1. *Endings*
                                               a. *ed* sound as "ed"

DIRECTIONS: In each row, draw a circle around the word ending with the **ed** sound.

1. jumped	wanted	showed
2. started	climbed	pushed
3. played	looked	planted
4. worked	filled	shouted
5. hunted	picked	laughed
6. pulled	danced	needed
7. heated	sawed	splashed
8. peeled	pasted	dropped

WORD ANALYSIS   B. Structural Analysis   1. *Endings*
                                              a. *ed* sound as "ed"

DIRECTIONS: Read each of the words. Circle **Yes** beside each word if you hear the **ed** sound at the end. Circle **No** if you do not hear the **ed** sound at the end.

1. needed   Yes   No

2. mopped   Yes   No

3. skated   Yes   No

4. cooked   Yes   No

5. played   Yes   No

6. painted   Yes   No

7. mixed   Yes   No

8. started   Yes   No

9. filled   Yes   No

10. dusted   Yes   No

WORD ANALYSIS   **B. Structural Analysis**   **1.** *Endings*
                                                   b. *ed* sound as "d"

DIRECTIONS: Trace over the words that end with the same **ed** sound as the key word.

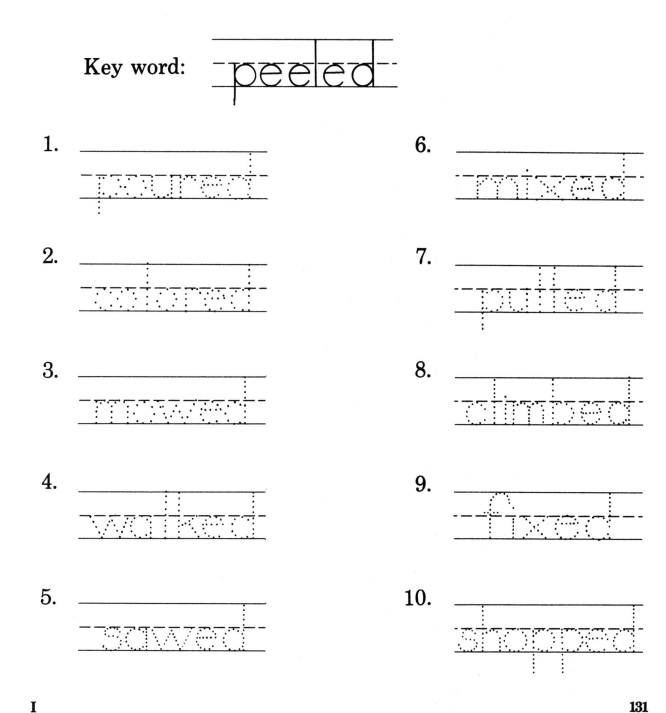

Key word: peeled

1. poured

2. colored

3. mowed

4. walked

5. sawed

6. mixed

7. pulled

8. climbed

9. fixed

10. stopped

WORD ANALYSIS   B. Structural Analysis   1. *Endings*
                                           b. *ed* sound as "d"

DIRECTIONS: In each sentence, draw a line under the word that ends with an **ed** but sounds like **d**. Write the word in the blank space.

1. The cat purred.
   jumped.

_____

5. Pat called Tom.
   splashed

_____

2. Sue dropped the milk.
   poured

_____

6. Mother baked the apple.
   peeled

_____

3. She fixed the wagon.
   pulled

_____

7. They planted the garden.
   watered

_____

4. Fred showed the picture.
   painted

_____

8. She played today.
   worked

_____

WORD ANALYSIS   B. Structural Analysis   1. *Endings*
                                             b. *ed* sound as "d"

DIRECTIONS: Draw a line under each word that ends with the sound of **d**.

1. baked	4. skipped	7. played
showed	poured	mixed
hated	washed	tapped
2. brushed	5. added	8. mowed
filled	stayed	walked
painted	dumped	milked
3. fixed	6. skipped	9. jumped
purred	killed	salted
hopped	dusted	lived

WORD ANALYSIS   **B. Structural Analysis**   1. *Endings*
                                                  b. *ed* sound as "d"

DIRECTIONS: Read each of the words. Circle **Yes** if the word ends with the **d** sound. Circle **No** if you do not hear the **d** sound.

1.	peeled	Yes	No
2.	lived	Yes	No
3.	dated	Yes	No
4.	splashed	Yes	No
5.	pulled	Yes	No
6.	dropped	Yes	No
7.	poured	Yes	No
8.	started	Yes	No
9.	filled	Yes	No
10.	colored	Yes	No

WORD ANALYSIS   **B. Structural Analysis**   *1. Endings*
                                                 c. *ed* sound as "t"

DIRECTIONS: Trace over the words that end with the same **ed** sound as in **jumped**.

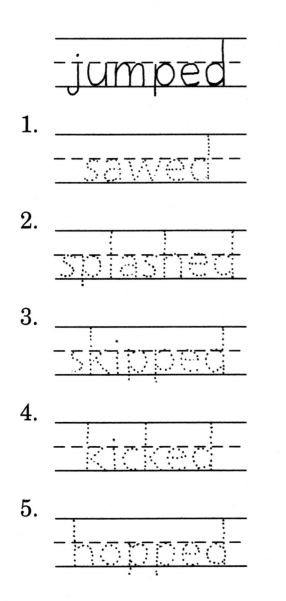
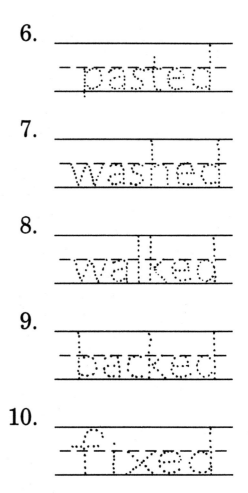

1. _sawed_

2. _splashed_

3. _skipped_

4. _kicked_

5. _hopped_

6. _pasted_

7. _washed_

8. _walked_

9. _backed_

10. _fixed_

WORD ANALYSIS   **B. Structural Analysis**   *1. Endings*
                                                     c. *ed* sound as "t"

DIRECTIONS: In each sentence, circle the word that ends with the **t** sound. Write the word in the space below the sentence.

1. Sam   played   on the farm.
          worked

_____

- - - - - - - - - - - - -

_____

2. They   climbed   the rope.
          jumped

_____

- - - - - - - - - - - - -

_____

3. Father   pushed   the box.
            pulled

_____

- - - - - - - - - - - - -

_____

4. Nell   fixed   the wagon.
          loaded

_____

- - - - - - - - - - - - -

_____

5. Beth   looked   at the book.
          stared

_____

- - - - - - - - - - - - -

_____

6. Mike   dropped   the glass.
          filled

_____

- - - - - - - - - - - - -

_____

7. The children   walked.
                  shouted.

_____

- - - - - - - - - - - - -

_____

8. The seals   splashed   in the water.
               played

_____

- - - - - - - - - - - - -

_____

WORD ANALYSIS   **B. Structural Analysis**   **1.** *Endings*
                                                 c. *ed* sound as "t"

DIRECTIONS: Draw a circle around each word that ends with **ed** but sounds like **t**.

A.

1. tricked
2. jumped
3. skated
4. splashed
5. cooked
6. hated
7. kicked
8. looked
9. pasted
10. peeled

B.

1. needed
2. helped
3. painted
4. hopped
5. started
6. worked
7. lived
8. pushed
9. farmed
10. mopped

WORD ANALYSIS   B. Structural Analysis   1. *Endings*
                                            c. *ed* sound as "t"

DIRECTIONS: Read each of the words. Circle **Yes** if the word ends with the **t** sound. Circle **No** if you do not hear the **t** sound at the end of the word.

1.	milked	Yes	No
2.	covered	Yes	No
3.	baked	Yes	No
4.	wished	Yes	No
5.	called	Yes	No
6.	hopped	Yes	No
7.	wanted	Yes	No
8.	skipped	Yes	No
9.	patted	Yes	No
10.	sawed	Yes	No

WORD ANALYSIS   B. Structural Analysis   2. *Compound words*

DIRECTIONS: In the box, draw a picture for each word. Make a compound word with the two small words. Write the word on the line next to the box.

1.   dog   house

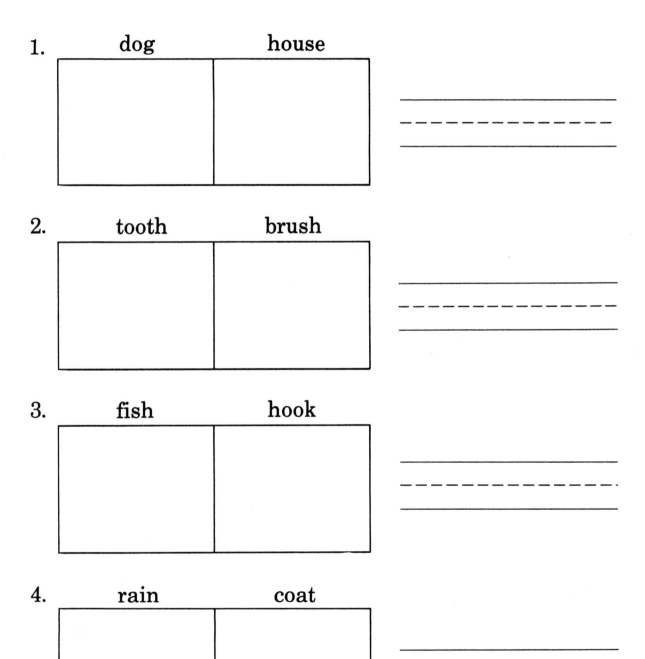

2.   tooth   brush

3.   fish   hook

4.   rain   coat

WORD ANALYSIS   B. Structural Analysis   2. *Compound words*

DIRECTIONS: Cut out the words in column B. Match the word in column A with a word in column B to make a compound word.

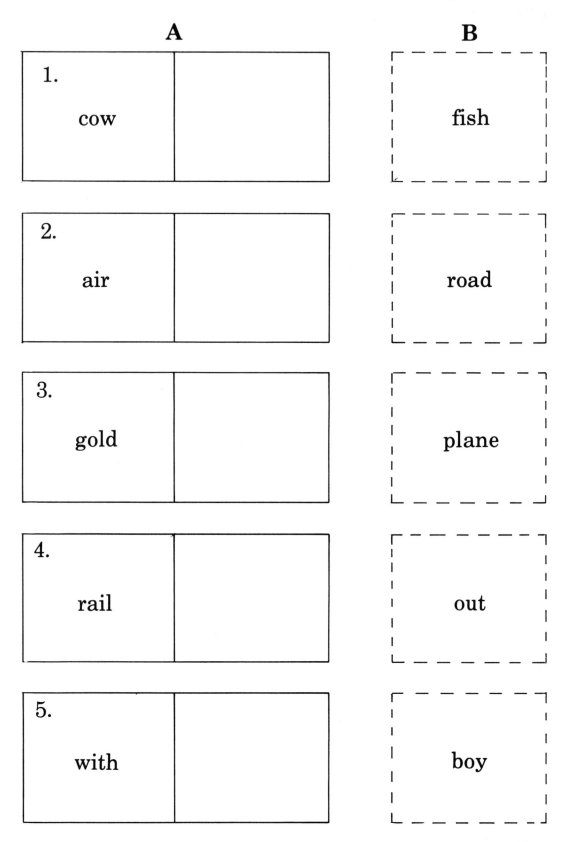

A   **B**

1. cow   fish

2. air   road

3. gold   plane

4. rail   out

5. with   boy

I

DIRECTIONS: Circle the compound word that best completes each sentence.

1. Kim wants a
   cannot.
   dollhouse.

2. They liked to play
   football.
   into.

3. Uncle Ned is a
   raincoat.
   policeman.

4. She went to see her
   grandmother.
   without.

5. The seesaw is at the
   playground.
   baseball.

6. Today is Sam's
   something.
   birthday.

7. Walk home on the
   sandbox.
   sidewalk.

WORD ANALYSIS   B. Structural Analysis   2. *Compound words*

DIRECTIONS: On the line, write the compound word that best completes each sentence.

1. A bell for a door is a _____ .
   doorbell   doormat

2. Light from the sun is called _____ .
   firelight   sunlight

3. A box for mail is a _____ .
   mailbag   mailbox

4. When a house is in a tree, it is a _____ .
   treehouse   treetop

5. Men who fight fires are called _____ .
   fireplace   firemen

6. If you work in the house, you are doing _____ .
   houseboat   housework

7. Drops of rain are called _____ .
   raindrops   rainbows

WORD ANALYSIS   **B. Structural Analysis**   **2. *Compound words***

DIRECTIONS: Read each compound word. Divide the word into the two smaller words that make up the compound word. Write the two words on the lines provided.

1. into   _____   _____

2. cowgirl   _____   _____

3. football   _____   _____

4. something   _____   _____

5. airplane   _____   _____

6. snowman   _____   _____

7. moonlight   _____   _____

8. bedroom   _____   _____

9. playhouse   _____   _____

10. railroad   _____   _____

DIRECTIONS: Read each compound word. Divide the word into the two smaller words that make up the compound word. Write the two words on the lines provided.

1. sidewalk   _____   _____

2. without   _____   _____

3. sunlight   _____   _____

4. birthday   _____   _____

5. cannot   _____   _____

6. grandmother   _____   _____

7. afternoon   _____   _____

8. buttermilk   _____   _____

9. sunflower   _____   _____

10. policeman   _____   _____

DIRECTIONS: Write one or more letters on the line that can go with the letters that are already there to make different words.

Example: _c_ all

_f_ all

_t_ all

1. ____ an

____ an

____ an

4. ____ at

____ at

____ at

7. ____ et

____ et

____ et

2. ____ ell

____ ell

____ ell

5. ____ ay

____ ay

____ ay

8. ____ ill

____ ill

____ ill

3. ____ ick

____ ick

____ ick

6. ____ it

____ it

____ it

9. ____ ing

____ ing

____ ing

WORD ANALYSIS   **B. Structural Analysis**   3. *Word families*

DIRECTIONS: Make word families by filling in a missing letter in front of the letters that are already there.

Example: __h__ ay

__s__ ay

__l__ ay

1. _____ ill

_____ ill

_____ ill

4. _____ am

_____ am

_____ am

7. _____ ish

_____ ish

_____ ish

2. _____ all

_____ all

_____ all

5. _____ ut

_____ ut

_____ ut

8. _____ it

_____ it

_____ it

3. _____ ed

_____ ed

_____ ed

6. _____ ip

_____ ip

_____ ip

9. _____ op

_____ op

_____ op

WORD ANALYSIS   B. Structural Analysis   3. *Word families*

DIRECTIONS: Make word families by writing a consonant in front of the parts of words. Say the word as you write it.

Example: _t_ in

_f_ in

_p_ in

1. ____ it   5. ____ ay   9. ____ amp

____ it   ____ ay   ____ amp

____ it   ____ ay   ____ amp

2. ____ ook   6. ____ ack   10. ____ ill

____ ook   ____ ack   ____ ill

____ ook   ____ ack   ____ ill

3. ____ at   7. ____ ip   11. ____ ake

____ at   ____ ip   ____ ake

____ at   ____ ip   ____ ake

4. ____ ish   8. ____ ell   12. ____ ing

____ ish   ____ ell   ____ ing

____ ish   ____ ell   ____ ing

WORD ANALYSIS   **B. Structural Analysis**   **3.** *Word families*

DIRECTIONS: On the line provided, write a consonant to make a rhyming word.

1. pan   ____ an

2. well   ____ ell

3. pay   ____ ay

4. sled   ____ ed

5. book   ____ ook

6. lamp   ____ amp

7. fish   ____ ish

8. rake   ____ ake

9. mop   ____ op

10. fast   ____ ast

11. pat   ____ at

12. nest   ____ est

13. hop   ____ op

14. sack   ____ ack

15. band   ____ and

I

WORD ANALYSIS   **C. Word Form Clues**   **1.** *Upper- and lower-case letters*

DIRECTIONS: Draw a circle around each upper-case letter. Put an X through each lower-case letter.

u	d	B	c	F	W	H
l	J	S	y	V	h	D
L	m	A	s	q	z	T
b	x	C	f	Q	M	R
t	E	k	n	I	v	G
Y	p	a	r	O	U	e

DIRECTIONS: Draw a line matching the upper- and lower-case words.

1.	red	can
2.	boy	Red
3.	Can	mat
4.	it	Boy
5.	Mat	It

6.	walk	Jump
7.	Funny	Walk
8.	jump	name
9.	Name	goat
10.	Goat	funny

11.	queen	Queen
12.	sit	Apple
13.	Tree	vest
14.	Vest	tree
15.	apple	Sit

DIRECTIONS: Draw a circle around the upper-case or capital letters.

a	i	R
B	j	S
c	K	T
d	L	u
E	m	v
F	n	W
g	O	x
H	P	Y
D	Q	Z

Draw a circle around the lower-case letters.

A	F	j	N	n	V	y
B	G	k	o	d	W	z
c	H	l	p	t	X	E
d	I	m	Q	V	e	f

DIRECTIONS: Write the correct word in each blank.

1. _____ rode a horse.
   (Dan, dan)

2. Her dog is named _____ .
   (tiger, Tiger)

3. _____ and _____ ate ice cream.
   (Carlos, carlos)   (i, I)

4. We went to visit _____ .
   (mike, Mike)

5. _____ and _____ want to go to the zoo.
   (nan, Nan)   (I, i)

6. The dog ran after _____ .
   (Queen, queen)

7. Did _____ and _____ go home?
   (gary, Gary)   (Ricky, ricky)

8. We had cake at the party for _____ .
   (Mark, mark)

9. _____ and _____ had fun at the fair.
   (ted, Ted)   (i, I)

10. She jumped rope with _____ and _____ .
    (Jim, jim)   (Will, will)

I

1. Draw a line under the lower-case letters.

R   a   D   J   Z   B   L   c   S   e   F   G   Y

U   m   H   o   V   I   p   T   w   K   x   n   Q

2. Circle the upper-case letters.

H   y   i   P   s   E   W   O   q   K   A   F   p   l

u   C   Z   m   T   j   x   b   R   g   v   N   D

3. Match the lower-case and upper-case letters.

j	k
K	Y
g	F
y	L
p	J
i	c
f	I
w	U
u	N
C	P
l	W
n	G

DIRECTIONS: In box A, write the lower-case letters. In box B, write the upper-case letters.

M   r   a   F   e   h   O   g   W   l   J

w   A   X   p   T   d   y   c   M   G   S

A	B
_____	_____
_____	_____
_____	_____
_____	_____
_____	_____
_____	_____
_____	_____
_____	_____
_____	_____
_____	_____

A.   DIRECTIONS: Circle the upper-case letters.

a   F   L   q   S   z   w   B   H

G   C   x   m   K   e   j   U   T

N   R   p   V   o   y   d   I   H

B.   DIRECTIONS: Write the lower-case letters for the following upper-case letters.

1. S _____   T _____   B _____   W _____

2. M _____   K _____   C _____   N _____

3. Y _____   D _____   I _____   E _____

4. O _____   F _____   L _____   Q _____

5. G _____   P _____   H _____   J _____

6. R _____   V _____   X _____   A _____

DIRECTIONS: Say each word in the box. Draw a circle around the longer word.

1. bat football	5. kitten fish	9. table car
2. sheep hippopotamus	6. cookies pie	10. grapes apple
3. jacket tie	7. bicycle boat	11. book pencil
4. bear monkey	8. jet tricycle	12. egg butter

WORD ANALYSIS   C. Word Form Clues   2. *Word length*

DIRECTIONS: Say each word in the box. Draw a circle around the longer word.

1. typewriter shirt	5. lipstick shirt	9. comb necklace
2. telephone ring	6. lamp flowers	10. basket three
3. television belt	7. key apple	11. basket three
4. piano shoe	8. brush pineapple	12. tiger bird

DIRECTIONS: Draw a circle around the longer word.

Example: house   (trailer)

Column A	Column B
1. cake	donut
2. umbrella	hat
3. whale	starfish
4. basketball	jacks
5. paper	pen
6. baby	boy
7. car	airplane
8. dog	handkerchief

WORD ANALYSIS   C. Word Form Clues   2. *Word length*

DIRECTIONS: Say the words in each row. If the first word is longer, draw a circle around the 1. If the second word is longer, draw a circle around the 2.

1. radio	cat	1	2
2. moon	fireman	1	2
3. guitar	plant	1	2
4. two	umbrella	1	2
5. gun	refrigerator	1	2
6. puppy	tire	1	2
7. star	mitten	1	2
8. purse	elephant	1	2

WORD ANALYSIS   C. Word Form Clues   3. *Double letters*

DIRECTIONS: In each box, circle the word that has double letters and draw a picture for the word.

1. hat ball	5. door ten
2. kitten ring	6. goat Daddy
3. bee cake	7. bike book
4. rabbit dish	8. bell jet

WORD ANALYSIS   C. Word Form Clues   3. *Double letters*

DIRECTIONS: Put an X through each word that has double letters.

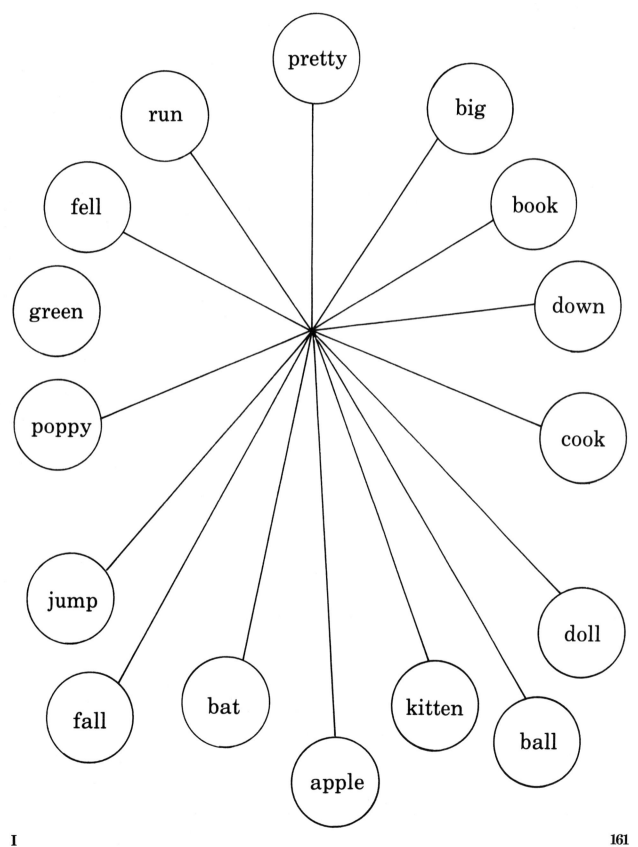

WORD ANALYSIS   C. Word Form Clues   3. *Double letters*

DIRECTIONS: In each row, draw a circle around the word that has double letters.

1. dress   help

2. hook   baby

3. Betty   black

4. car   jeep

5. zoo   house

6. girl   puppy

7. three   water

8. smell   me

9. bunny   hair

10. need   cow

WORD ANALYSIS   C. Word Form Clues   3. *Double letters*

DIRECTIONS: Draw a circle around each word that has double letters.

Column A	Column B
tall	soon
let	little
penny	apple
head	orange
seed	tennis
read	yellow
took	blue
Larry	tree
five	today
sleep	me
pill	room
dime	puppy

COMPREHENSION   A. Symbolic Representation

DIRECTIONS: Name the picture in each box and tell your teacher something about it.

Name: _____ Date: _____

DIRECTIONS: Read the sentences. Draw a picture in each box about the sentence. Write a word that tells about your picture on the line.

1. This is my favorite food. _____	2. This is what I want to be when I grow up. _____
3. This is what I like to do best at school. _____	4. This makes me very happy. _____

I

COMPREHENSION   **A. Symbolic Representation**

DIRECTIONS: Draw a picture about the word in each box.

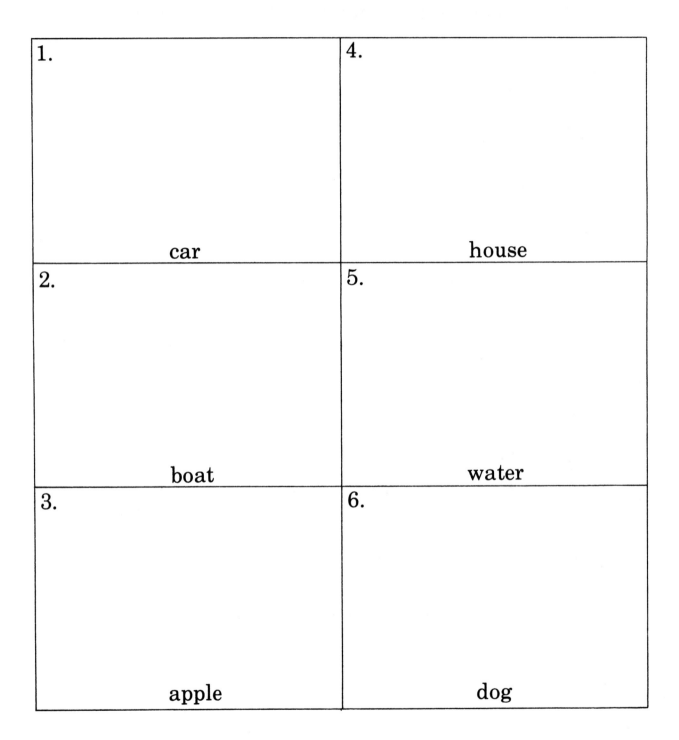

1.	4.
car	house
2.	5.
boat	water
3.	6.
apple	dog

COMPREHENSION   A. Symbolic Representation

DIRECTIONS: Cut out the words in the boxes on the right. Paste each word beside the correct picture.

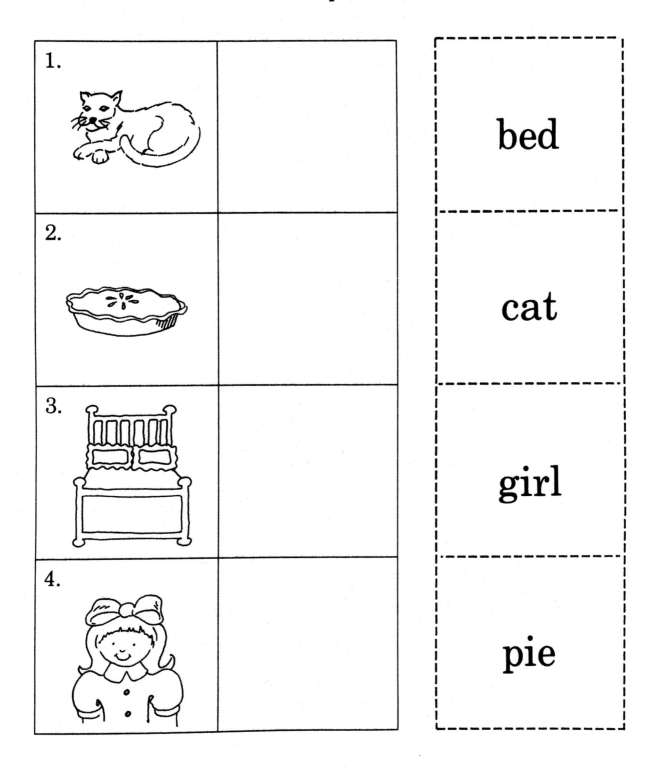

Name: _____ Date: _____

DIRECTIONS: Cut out the words in the boxes on the right. Paste each word beside the correct picture.

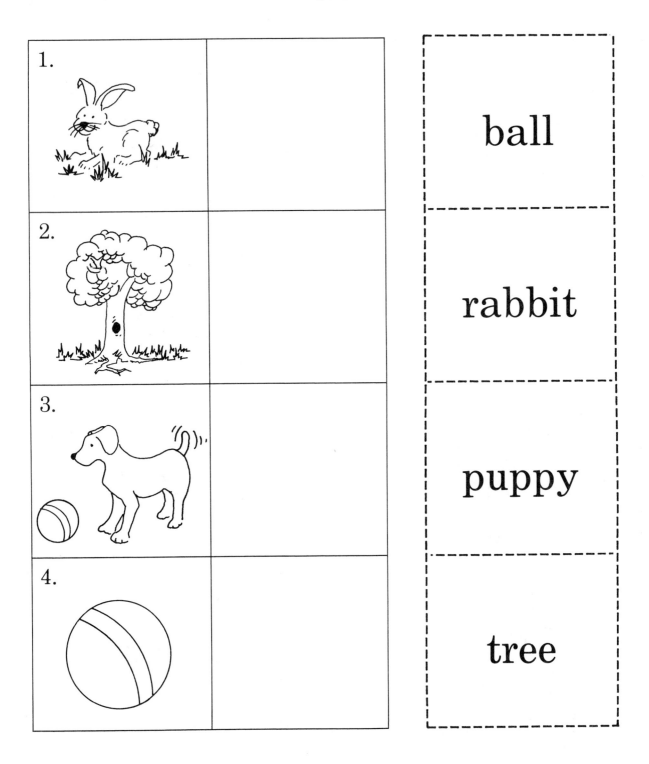

I

COMPREHENSION   **A. Symbolic Representation**

TEACHER DIRECTIONS: Cut out the flashcards below. Paste them on 1¾″ × 6¾″ oaktag strips. Show each word and picture to the children. Let them dramatize the words on the cards. When children have become familiar with the words, cut each card in the middle and paste the back sides together. The children can practice dramatizing the words and they can check their responses by looking at the picture on the back of each word card.

	splash
	laugh
	read
	eat

COMPREHENSION   B. Following Printed Directions

DIRECTIONS: **Read the sentences and follow the directions.**

1. Color the balloon red.

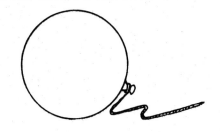

2. Color the dog black.

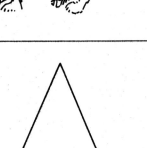

3. Color the triangle blue.

4. Color the rectangle yellow.

5. Color the circle green.

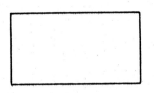

Name: _____ Date: _____

COMPREHENSION   B. Following Printed Directions

DIRECTIONS: Read the sentences and follow the directions.

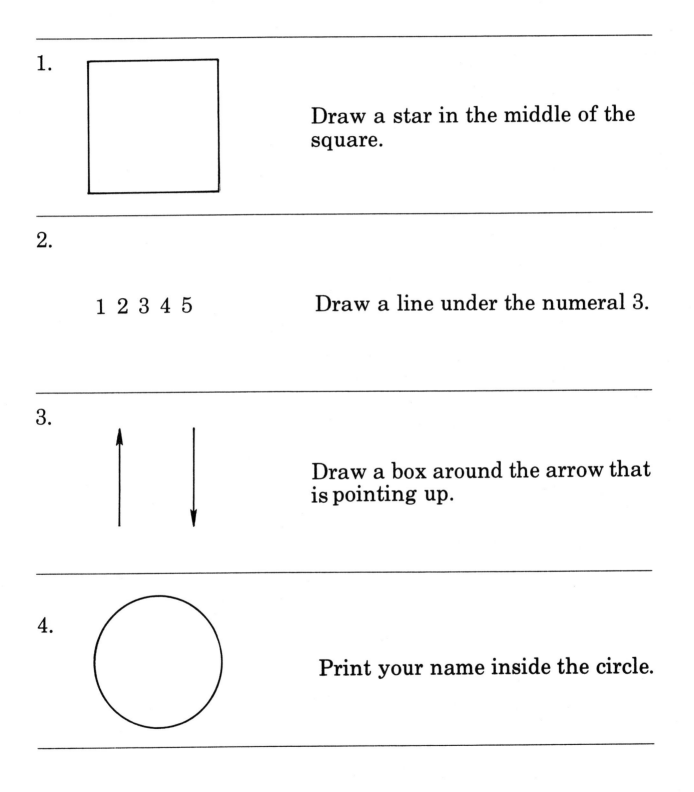

1.   Draw a star in the middle of the square.

2.   1 2 3 4 5   Draw a line under the numeral 3.

3.   Draw a box around the arrow that is pointing up.

4.   Print your name inside the circle.

COMPREHENSION   **B. Following Printed Directions**

DIRECTIONS: Read each sentence and follow the directions.

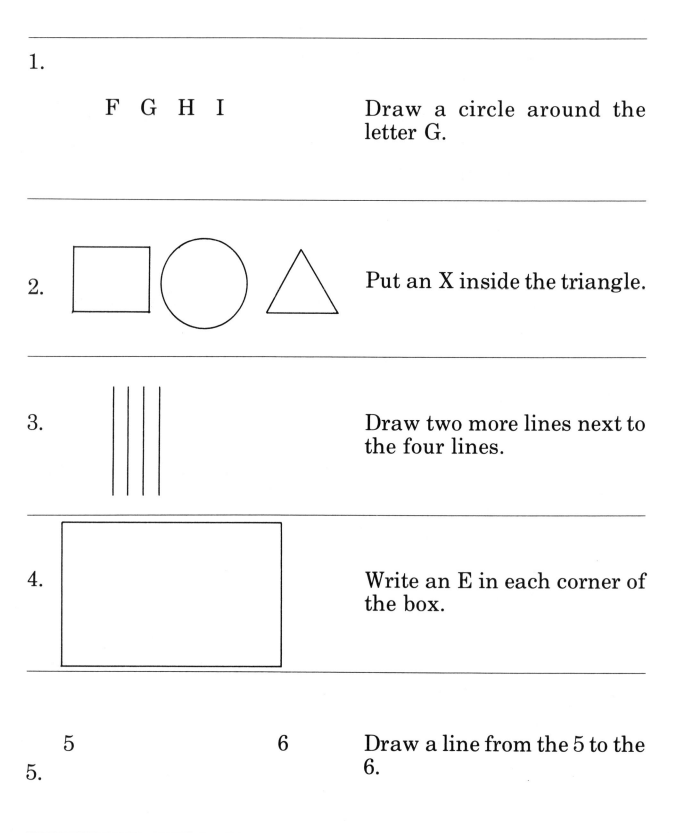

1.

    F G H I   Draw a circle around the letter G.

2.   Put an X inside the triangle.

3.   Draw two more lines next to the four lines.

4.   Write an E in each corner of the box.

    5   6   Draw a line from the 5 to the 6.

5.

COMPREHENSION   B. Following Printed Directions

DIRECTIONS: Read the sentences and follow the directions.

1. Print the letter A and draw a line under it.

2. Draw an apple and color it red.

3. Draw a triangle. Put an X above it.

4. Write the numerals from 1 to 10. Draw a circle around the numeral 3.

5. Draw six balls. Color three of them blue. Color three of them green.

COMPREHENSION   B. Following Printed Directions

DIRECTIONS: Read the sentences and follow the directions.

1. Draw a square. Draw a circle inside the square.

2. Draw a happy face and write your name under it.

3. Write the numerals 1 through 7. Draw a circle around the numeral 1. Draw a line under the numeral 5.

4. Draw a rectangle. Write the letter A above the rectangle.

5. Draw a star. Put an X below the star.

COMPREHENSION   C. Drawing Conclusions

DIRECTIONS: Look at the picture. Answer the questions at the bottom of the page.

1. What kind of a party is it? _____

2. Who is having a birthday party? _____

3. How old is he? _____

4. Did he receive any presents? _____

5. What will the children eat? _____

6. Is the party inside or outside? _____

COMPREHENSION   C. Drawing Conclusions

DIRECTIONS: Draw a line under the correct picture.

1. Kenya ate a _____ for lunch.

2. Mother drives the _____ to work.

3. Carol looked up and saw a bright _____ in the sky.

4. Chang went outside to play on the _____ .

5. Ben put on a _____ at the Halloween party.

Name: _____ Date: _____

COMPREHENSION   C. Drawing Conclusions

DIRECTIONS: Read the sentences in the boxes. Cut out the pictures at the bottom of the page. Paste each picture in the correct box.

1. Jack likes toy airplanes. He worked and got some money. He went to the store. What did Jack buy?	
2. Joe was playing outside. He was on a team. He had a bat. What was Joe going to hit?	
3. Linda was hungry. She went to the kitchen. She got something red. What did Linda eat?	
4. Mary had to go to school. She had to walk. It was raining. What did Mary get?	

I

COMPREHENSION   C. Drawing Conclusions   I

DIRECTIONS: Read the words and sentences below. On each blank line, write the word that tells how the child felt.

sick   hungry   tired   hurt   sad

1.   Tom was riding his bike.
      It fell over.
      Tom's leg was cut.

      Tom was _____ .

2.   Carlos had a dog.
      The dog ran away.
      Carlos missed him very much.

      Carlos was _____ .

3.   Jan's mother cooked dinner.
      Jan did not eat.
      Later she went to the kitchen.

      Jan was _____ .

4.   Mike had a cold.
      He did not feel well.
      He went to the doctor.

      Mike was _____ .

5.   Kim played outside.
      She ran, skipped, and jumped.
      Then she sat down.

      Kim was _____ .

COMPREHENSION   C. Drawing Conclusions

DIRECTIONS: Write the answer to each riddle. Draw a picture beside each riddle about the answer.

1.   I have four legs.
      I have a tail.
      I can bark.
      I do not like cats.

      I am a _____ .

2.   I have wings.
      I fly in the sky.
      I go to many towns and cities.
      People ride inside me.

      I am a _____ .

3.   I live in the water.
      My fins help me swim.
      I like to eat worms.
      People like to catch me.

      I am a _____ .

4.   I am in the sky.
      I am big and round.
      I am yellow and I shine.
      You see me during the day.

      I am the _____ .

I

COMPREHENSION   D. Recall from Stories Read Aloud   1. *Main idea*

DIRECTIONS: Read the story aloud and then draw a picture about the story at the bottom of the page.

Jan's First Train Ride

Jan and her mother got on the train. They were going to visit Jan's grandmother in the country. "I am very happy, Mother," said Jan. "This is the first time I have ever been on a train." The train was very long. It had a big engine in the front and a red caboose at the end. "Trains are fun to ride on," said Mother. "You will have a good time on your first trip on a train."

COMPREHENSION   D. Recall from Stories Read Aloud   1. *Main idea*

DIRECTIONS: Read each story aloud, and then read the three sentences under the story. Put an X by the sentence that tells the main idea of the story.

Dan wanted a pet. Tom's dog had puppies. Dan liked one of the puppies best. He was brown. The puppy played with Dan when he came to Tom's house. Dan asked Tom if he could have the puppy.

_____ 1. Dan wanted one of Tom's puppies.

_____ 2. Tom had kittens at his house.

_____ 3. Dan wanted a bird.

Tim and Sam went to the zoo. They saw many animals. The bears were asleep. The elephant had a new baby. They laughed at the monkeys. Tim liked the tigers best. Sam liked the snakes best of all.

_____ 1. Tim and Sue went to the pet shop.

_____ 2. Sam went to the fair.

_____ 3. Tim and Sam saw many animals at the zoo.

DIRECTIONS: Read each story aloud and then read the titles under each story. Put an X by the best title for each story.

Bill lives on a farm. Bill helps his mother and father do the work. He feeds the pigs and chickens. He milks Betsy the cow. Sometimes Father lets him drive the tractor. Bill helps his mother work in the garden. There is a lot of work to do on a farm.

_____ 1. Bill and His Father

_____ 2. Bill Helps on the Farm

_____ 3. Cows and Chickens

Sam and Mike went fishing. They went to the pond near Sam's house. They sat and sat. Mike's pole began to move. He felt something pulling on the line. "Sam," said Mike, "I think I have a fish!" Sam helped him pull the fish out of the water. Mike and Sam smiled. "This is the biggest fish we have ever caught!" said Sam.

_____ 1. Sam Went to the Store

_____ 2. A Big Fish

_____ 3. The Pond

DIRECTIONS: Read each story aloud. Draw a line under the sentence that is the main idea in each story.

1. Mike and Joe like to play baseball. After school they play at the ball field. Their team is named the Tigers. Mike is the pitcher. Joe plays first base. Sometimes their team wins, but sometimes the Tigers lose. Mike and Joe want to be baseball players when they grow up.

2. Sue likes to go to the library. "Mother," asked Sue, "May I go to the library today?" Mother smiled. "Yes, Sue. I will go with you." Sue got two books to read. The lady at the library read her a story. "It is time to go now, Sue," said Mother. Sue waved to the lady in the library. "I will be back soon," she said.

3. Fred had a birthday party. Many of his friends came. They ate cake and ice cream. Fred's big brother played games with them. Everyone got a prize. Fred got some birthday presents. He got a math game, a toy truck, and a jump rope. He thanked his friends for the nice presents. Everyone had a good time.

I

DIRECTIONS: Read each story aloud. Then, read the three sentences under each story. Put an X by the sentence that tells the main idea of the story.

Did you know that the sun is really a star? It looks bigger than the other stars because it is so much closer to us. But it is really just another star.

Since the sun is closer to us than the other stars, we use the heat and light that the sun gives off. It keeps us warm and helps plants grow. Without the heat and the light from the sun, there could be no food, animals, or people.

1. _____ The sun looks bigger than the other stars.

2. _____ We need the heat and the light from the sun to live.

3. _____ The sun is closer to us than the other stars.

If you have red, yellow, and blue paint, you can mix them to make different colors. Red and yellow paint mixed together will give you orange paint. If you mix the colors blue and yellow, the paint will turn green. You can make purple paint by mixing the colors red and blue. Mixing paint to make new colors can be fun.

1. _____ You can make new colors by mixing different colors of paint.

2. _____ If you mix red and yellow paint, the paint will turn orange.

3. _____ Painting pictures is fun.

DIRECTIONS: Read the story aloud and then read the questions below the story. Cut out the names at the bottom of the page. Paste each name by the question it answers.

Jan Smith was a new girl in town. She did not have any friends. Mary Martin lived in the house next to Jan. One day Mary went to play with Jan. Sherry Jones lived down the street. When she saw Mary and Jan outside, she went to play with them. The three girls had a good time playing. Jan made two good friends in one day.

1. Who was the new girl in town?

2. Who lived down the street from Jan?

3. Who lived next door to Jan?

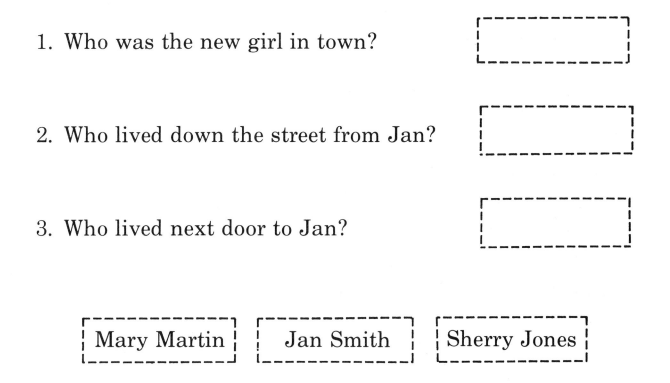

Mary Martin   Jan Smith   Sherry Jones

DIRECTIONS: **Read the sentences aloud and write the answers to the questions on the lines.**

1. Mark went to the store with his mother.
   Who went to the store with his mother?

   _____

2. Susie wants to be a doctor when she grows up.
   Who wants to be a doctor when she grows up?

   _____

3. Kevin played outside in the snow with Mike.
   Who played outside in the snow with Mike?

   _____

4. Mr. Smith got Brad a horse for his birthday.
   Who got a horse for his birthday?

   _____

5. Nan's softball team won the game.
   Whose team won the softball game?

   _____

6. Sally lives in an apartment in the city.
   Who lives in an apartment in the city?

   _____

7. Uncle Joe sings in a band.
   Who sings in a band?

   _____

Name: _____ Date: _____

DIRECTIONS: Read the story aloud and then draw a picture at the bottom of this sheet of all of the animals in the story.

Once there was a frog named Sam and a mouse named Tom. They lived by a big pond deep in the woods. One day a new animal came to the woods. She was a small black ant named Nelly. Sam, Tom, and Nelly became good friends. They played every day in the tall green grass that grew around the pond.

DIRECTIONS: Read the story aloud. Then read the questions below the story. Draw a line from each question to the correct answer.

Maria goes to King Elementary School. Maria's teacher's name is Mrs. Green. Mrs. Green is very nice. All of the children like her. Maria's best friend is also in Mrs. Green's class. Her name is Betsy. They work and play together at school. Betsy and Maria live on Oak Street. After school they play together. Sometimes Betsy's little sister plays with them. Her name is Carla.

1. What is Maria's teacher's name?

Mrs. Green

Miss Hill

2. Who is Maria's best friend?

Betsy

Carla

3. What is Betsy's little sister's name?

Susie

Carla

DIRECTIONS: Read the story aloud. Then answer the questions below the story.

Tom's father is a fireman. His name is Mr. Parks. One day Mr. Parks told Tom that he could bring two of his friends to the fire station. Tom asked Fred and Mark to go. They got to sit on the fire truck and ring the bell. Mr. Parks showed them the things firemen use to put out fires. The boys also met the fire chief. His name is Mr. Young. Mark said that he wants to be a fireman when he grows up.

1. What is Tom's father's name? _____

2. Which boys went with Tom to the fire station?_____

   and _____

3. What is the fire chief's name? _____

4. Who wants to be a fireman when he grows up? _____

DIRECTIONS: Read the sentences aloud and write the answers to the questions on the blank lines.

1. Fred got a new truck at the toy store.
   What did Fred get at the toy store?

   _____

2. Mr. Wong is the art teacher at Hill Elementary School.
   Where does Mr. Wong teach art?

   _____

3. Tom's class goes to music on Wednesday mornings.
   What day does Tom's class go to music?

   _____

4. Mother made Sally a red dress to wear to school.
   What color is the dress Mother made for Sally?

   _____

5. The zoo got two new baby goats for the petting zoo.
   How many new baby goats did the zoo get?

   _____

6. Kay lives on a farm with her grandmother and grandfather.
   Where does Kay live?

   _____

7. Daddy went to the library and got three books to read.
   How many books did Daddy get at the library?

   _____

DIRECTIONS: Read the story aloud. Then read the sentences below the story. Draw a happy face after each sentence that is true. Draw a sad face after each sentence that is not true.

Tommy wanted to go outside to play. He could not because it was raining. "I'm sorry you cannot go outside," said Mother. "You will have to play inside today." Tommy got his jacks. He and Mother played jacks on the living room floor. Next he got his crayons and paper. He drew a picture of his house. He wrote his name on it and gave it to his mother. "Tommy," said Mother, "what a pretty picture! I will put it on the wall." Then Tommy helped Mother make a snack. Tommy had fun helping Mother in the kitchen. "Rainy days can be fun days," said Tommy.

1. Tommy could not go outside because it was raining.

2. Tommy played jacks on the kitchen floor.

3. Tommy drew a picture of his green bike.

4. Mother put Tommy's picture on the wall.

5. Tommy helped Mother make a snack.

DIRECTIONS: Read the story aloud. Then read the questions below the story. Draw a picture to show the answer to each question.

Sammy woke up one morning. He heard noises outside. He got out of bed and looked out the window. The sun was up and shining. He heard something singing, "Chirp, chirp." It was a bird singing in the oak tree. A dog was barking, "Bow wow!" It was Spot. He was running after a cat. The cat was screaming, "Meow! Meow!" Sammy heard another noise. It was his baby brother crying. Sammy said, "It is time for me to get up. It is too noisy for me to sleep!"

1. Was it a sunny or a rainy day?	2. What was singing in the oak tree?
3. What was Spot running after?	4. Who was crying?

DIRECTIONS: Read the story aloud. Then read the questions below the story. Write the answer to each question on the line.

Doug went to the library. He checked out two books. One book was about race cars. The name of the book was Fast Cars. It was a big book and had pictures of race cars in it. The other book Doug took out was a cookbook. It showed how to make some good things to eat. Before he left, the lady at the library read The Three Little Pigs to him. Her name was Mrs. Brown.

1. Where did Doug go? _____

2. How many books did Doug take from the library?

_____

3. What was the name of the race car book?

_____

4. What kind of book was the other book that Doug got?

_____

5. What story did the lady at the library read?

_____

6. What was the lady's name? _____

COMPREHENSION   D. Recall from Stories Read Aloud   3. *Details*

DIRECTIONS: Read the story aloud. Then read the sentences below it. On the line write the correct word to complete each sentence.

Plants can do something that animals and people cannot do. They can make their own food. A plant has three parts that help it make its own food. They are the leaves, the stem, and the roots.

The roots take in the water a plant needs from the ground. The plant sends the water through its stem to the leaves. Gas from the air is taken in through the leaves. Then, when the sun shines on the plant, it mixes the gas and the water to make its own food.

1. Plants can make their own (water food sun). _____

2. The three parts of a plant that help it make its own food are the leaves, the stem, and the (gas air roots). _____

3. A plant takes in (water leaves food) through its roots.

   _____

4. The water goes from the roots, through the stem, and then to the (air ground leaves). _____

5. When the sun shines on the plant, it mixes the water and the (roots gas leaves) to make its food. _____

COMPREHENSION   **D. Recall from Stories Read Aloud**   **4. *Sequence***

DIRECTIONS: Read each sentence aloud. Then write the answer to each question on the line.

A. Tom went to the park. When he came back, he went to Fred's house.

    1. Where did Tom go first? _____

    _____

    2. Then where did Tom go? _____

    _____

B. Mary read a book. Later she went outside to play.

    1. What did Mary do first? _____

    _____

    2. Then what did Mary do? _____

    _____

C. Sam cleaned his room. Then he did his homework.

    1. What did Sam do first? _____

    _____

    2. What did Sam do next? _____

    _____

DIRECTIONS: Read the story aloud. Then cut out the sentences at the bottom of the page. Paste the sentences in the boxes to show the order in which they happened.

It was time for Mother to cook dinner. "Mother," said Tim, "I will help you." First, Tim and Mother put the dishes on the table. Then they cooked the food. They laughed and talked as they worked. The last thing they did was put the food on the table. "Tim," said Mother, "you made cooking dinner fun."

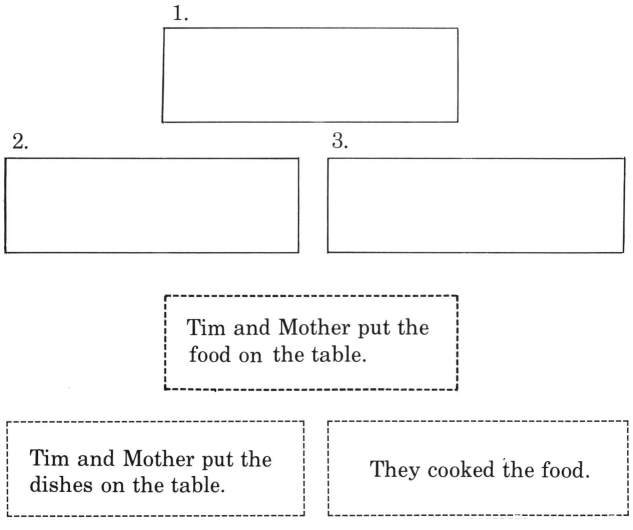

1.

2.

3.

Tim and Mother put the food on the table.

Tim and Mother put the dishes on the table.

They cooked the food.

COMPREHENSION   **D. Recall from Stories Read Aloud**   *4. Sequence*

DIRECTIONS: Read the story aloud. Then write the answer to each question below on the lines.

Maria went for a walk along the beach. As she began her walk, she found different kinds of shells. Many were colored gold, pink, or white. Some of the shells were striped.

As Maria kept walking down the beach, she saw some seaweed plants. These plants had been washed up on the beach from the ocean floor. One seaweed Maria saw was dry and brown. Another seaweed was long and green. She even saw red and purple seaweed plants.

On her way home, Maria found an old piece of gray wood. She thought that it might be from a large ship from long, long ago.

Maria enjoyed her walk along the beach. She had seen many interesting things.

1. The first thing Maria saw on the beach were some

_____.

2. Next, Maria found some _____.

3. The last thing she found was _____.

DIRECTIONS: Read the story aloud. Then read the sentences below the story. Number the sentences from 1 to 4 to show the order in which they happened.

"Today is a pretty spring day," said Kim. "I will go riding on my bike." The grass was green. New leaves were on the trees. She saw a bird building its nest. There were many different kinds of flowers in the yards. Bees were flying around some of the flowers. She saw Mr. Chin mowing his grass. On her way back home, she saw some boys and girls playing ball. "My," said Kim, "spring is a busy time of year!"

_____ Kim saw a bird building its nest.

_____ She saw Mr. Chin mowing his grass.

_____ Kim went riding on her bike.

_____ She saw some children playing ball.

DIRECTIONS: Read the story aloud. Then read the sentences below the story. Number the sentences from 1 to 5 to show the order in which they happened.

Mother took Carol to the dentist. The dentist's name was Dr. Jones. "Good morning, Carol," said Dr. Jones. "I am glad you came to visit me today." Dr. Jones smiled and said, "Open your mouth very wide." She looked inside Carol's mouth. Dr. Jones cleaned Carol's teeth. She gave Carol a new toothbrush. She showed Carol the best way to brush her teeth. "You have a pretty smile," said Dr. Jones. "I want you to keep it."

_____ Dr. Jones showed Carol how to brush her teeth.

_____ Carol went to visit the dentist.

_____ The dentist gave Carol a new toothbrush.

_____ Dr. Jones cleaned Carol's teeth.

_____ Dr. Jones told Carol that she had a pretty smile.

COMPREHENSION   E. Recall After Silent Reading   1. *Main idea*

DIRECTIONS: Read the story. Draw a picture about the story at the bottom of the page.

Mark had a Halloween party at his house. Everyone was dressed in a funny costume. Some of the children had paint on their faces. Dan and Tim were wearing masks. The children played games and sang Halloween songs. Mr. Smith told them a story about witches. Mrs. Smith had apples, popcorn, and cookies for them to eat. Everyone had a good time at Mark's Halloween party.

DIRECTIONS: Read each story. Draw a line under the sentence in each story that best tells the main idea of the story.

1.   Sue got a new bicycle for her birthday. It is blue with white stripes. There is a basket on the front. It also has a horn. Sue takes good care of her new birthday present.

2.   Grandfather and Dan went to the zoo. The walked and walked. They saw a big tiger. Some of the animals looked mean. Some of the animals looked funny. Dan liked the elephants the best. Grandfather liked the bears the best. Grandfather and Dan want to go back to the zoo.

3.   It was a warm Saturday morning. Joe and Buddy went fishing. They went to the pond by the park. They took their fishing poles and some worms. They fished until it was time for lunch. Joe caught three big catfish. Buddy only got one fish. They had a good time.

DIRECTIONS: Cut out the two titles at the bottom of this page. Paste each title above the correct story.

1.

Sue has a playhouse in her back yard. Sue, Mary, and Carla went to the playhouse. They played with their dolls. Then they ate cookies and drank milk. Mary colored a picture. Carla and Sue made snakes with clay. They had fun at the playhouse.

2.

"I have a surprise for you," said Daddy. "I put something in this box." Andy asked, "May I look in the box now? I want to see what is inside." Daddy smiled. "Yes," he said. "Go ahead and open it." Andy took the top off the box. "Oh!" Andy said. A big frog jumped out. Andy laughed and said, "Daddy, I like your surprise!"

A Surprise for Andy   At the Playhouse

Name: _____   Date: _____

DIRECTIONS: Read each story. Read the three sentences below each story. Put an X by the sentence that tells about the story.

Tom went to see his grandfather who lives on a farm. Grandfather let Tom help milk the cow. They fed the chickens and the pigs. Tom got to ride a horse. His name was Bud. Tom likes to go to his grandfather's house.

_____ 1. Tom went to the store with his grandfather.

_____ 2. Tom went to the zoo with his grandfather.

_____ 3. Tom went to his grandfather's farm.

Kim is four years old. She goes to school. Mrs. Tate is her teacher. She reads good books to Kim and her friends. Sometimes Mrs. Tate lets them paint pictures, sing songs, and play games. Every Friday they cook something. Kim likes to play outside the best.

_____ 1. Mrs. Tate is Kim's mother.

_____ 2. Kim does many things at school.

_____ 3. Kim has fun at home with Mrs. Tate.

COMPREHENSION   E. Recall After Silent Reading   1. *Main idea*

DIRECTIONS: Read the story. Read the sentences below the story. Put an X by the sentence that tells the main idea of the story.

If you were in a rocket flying in space, you could see many interesting things. If you saw earth, it would look round like a ball. You could see the earth's land and water. Around the earth you would see many clouds.

From your rocket you could see a much smaller ball moving around the earth. The ball would be the earth's moon. You could watch the moon as it moved in its path around the earth once every month.

If you were in space, you could also see the earth turn around the sun. But you would have to stay in your rocket for a whole year to see the earth move around the sun one time.

There are many other things to see in space. Maybe some day you will be able to see them as you ride through space in a rocket.

_____   1. The earth turns around the sun once a year.

_____   2. If you could look at the earth from a rocket in space, it would look like a ball.

_____   3. If you were in a rocket in space, you could see many interesting things.

_____   4. The moon moves around the earth.

COMPREHENSION   E. Recall After Silent Reading   2. *Characters*

DIRECTIONS: Read the sentences. Answer the question after each sentence.

1. Nan helped her Mother with the dishes.
   Who helped her Mother with the dishes? _____

2. The boy who hit the home run was Mark.
   Who hit the home run? _____

3. Tim is Sally's little brother.
   Who is Sally's little brother? _____

4. The winner of the game was Sam.
   Who was the winner of the game? _____

5. Fred rode Ted's horse.
   Who rode Ted's horse? _____

6. Pat and Carl are brothers.
   Who is Pat's brother? _____

7. Ned can play the drums.
   Who can play the drums? _____

DIRECTIONS: Read the story. Read the questions below the story. Draw a line from each question to the correct answer.

Sammy went to the playground with Ken. Mary and Cathy were playing on the swings. Mike and Sue were playing on the seesaw. Fred was building a house in the sandbox. Kim was playing on the monkey bars. Sammy and Ken went to slide down the sliding board. All of the children were having a good time at the playground.

---

1. Who went to the playground with Ken?

Sammy

Mary

---

2. Which children were playing on the swings?

Mike and Sue

Mary and Cathy

---

3. Who was building a house in the sandbox?

Fred

Mike

---

4. Who went to slide down the sliding board?

Sammy and Ken

Sue and Cathy

DIRECTIONS: Read the story. Write the correct answer to each question below the story.

Mr. Lopez took Pedro and some of his friends on a trip to the woods. Ben saw some footprints in the dirt. Close to the footprints he saw a hole in the ground. Mr. Lopez said, "These are a rabbit's tracks, and the hole must go to his home."

Mr. Lopez and the boys walked deeper into the woods. Nicky pointed to a large nest in a tree. "I bet squirrels live up there," he said. "The nest is too large to be a bird's nest." Mr. Lopez said, "I believe you are right, Nicky. That nest may be the home of a mother squirrel and her babies."

"Listen," said Mark. "I hear something tapping. What could it be?" They walked very quietly. The tapping became louder and louder. "Look!" said Pedro. "It's a woodpecker tapping the tree with its beak."

"Our walk in the woods today has been fun," said Mr. Lopez. "We will have to take another trip soon."

1. Who took the boys on a trip to the woods? _____
   (Mr. Nichols   Mr. Lopez   Mrs. Martin)
2. Which boy saw the rabbit's tracks and the hole in the

   ground? _____ (Pedro   Mark   Ben)

3. Who saw the squirrel's nest? _____
   (Mr. Lopez   Nicky   Pedro)
4. Who heard the tapping noise? _____
   (Mark   Ben   Mr. Lopez)
5. Which boy saw the woodpecker? _____
   (Nicky   Ben   Pedro)

DIRECTIONS: Read the story. Read the sentences below the story. Draw a happy face by each sentence that is true. Draw a sad face by each sentence that is not true.

Mr. Martin and his class gave a play for the school. The children were dressed like people or animals in stories they liked. Nancy was dressed like a witch. Nick looked like Humpty Dumpty. Mary and Ted were dressed like rabbits. Mark was the funniest. He was dressed like a big fat clown. Andy, Tommy, and Carol looked like sheep. They painted their faces and wore white clothes. Everyone had fun.

1. Mr. Smith's class gave a play for the school.

2. Jean was dressed like a witch.

3. Nick looked like Humpty Dumpty.

4. Mary and Ted were dressed like rabbits.

5. Fred looked like a clown.

6. Andy, Carol, and Tommy were dressed like white sheep.

Name: _____ Date: _____

DIRECTIONS: Read the story. Read the questions and words below the story. Draw a line from each question to the right name.

Pat's family had a picnic in her back yard. Mother put the dishes and napkins on the table. Pat made the iced tea. Daddy cooked the hot dogs. Aunt Nell baked some beans. Pat's big brother went to the store and got some potato chips. When Grandfather came, he made ice cream. Pat's family had a good time at the picnic.

1. Who put out the dishes and napkins?   Pat

2. Who made the ice cream?   Mother

3. Who cooked the hot dogs?   Daddy

4. Who got the potato chips?   Pat's big brother

5. Who baked the beans?   Grandfather

6. Who made the iced tea?   Aunt Nell

DIRECTIONS: Read the sentences. Answer the question after each sentence.

1. Mike made a snake out of clay.
   What did Mike make out of clay?   _____

2. Nancy will be seven years old on
   her birthday.
   How old will Nancy be on her
   birthday?   _____

3. On Saturday, Father went fishing
   with the children.
   When did Father and the children
   go fishing?   _____

4. At the store, Mary got two pieces
   of candy.
   How many pieces of candy did Mary
   get?   _____

5. Tim lives on Main Street.
   Where does Tim live?   _____

6. Sally made her mother a pretty
   card for Mother's Day.
   What did Sally make for her
   mother?   _____

7. The new boy at school is Mark
   Brown.
   Who is the new boy at school?   _____

DIRECTIONS: Read the story. Read the questions below the story. Draw a picture to show the answer to each question.

Miss Williams took the class outside to play. "Today is free play day," said Miss Williams. "You may play anything you want." Some of the children wanted to play softball. Tim got a ball and bat. Cathy and Sue played basketball with a large ball. Pat got three jump ropes for some of her friends. Fred and Sam played jacks under a tree.

1. What did Cathy and Sue play?	2. How many jump ropes did Pat get?
3. What two things did Tim get to play softball?	4. Where did Fred and Sam play jacks?

DIRECTIONS: Read the story. Read the questions below the story. Draw a line from each question to the correct answer.

Kim had a birthday party at her house. Mother got her a big white cake. It had seven pink candles. Mother also made pink punch for the children to drink. Many of Kim's friends came to her party. They played games inside the house. The winner of each game won a small book. Mother gave Kim a new doll for her birthday present. The doll wore a pretty red dress. She talked when you pulled a string. Kim had a good time at her birthday party.

---

1. Where did Kim have her birthday party?

at her house

at the park

---

2. How old was Kim?

six years old

seven years old

---

3. What did the winner of each game get?

a toy truck

a small book

---

4. What color was the new doll's dress?

red

blue

DIRECTIONS: Read the story. Answer the questions after the story.

Mark went to the store with his grandmother. "Grandmother," said Mark, "today I will help you with the shopping." Mark pushed the shopping cart. Grandmother got a ham to cook for dinner. "Mark," said Grandmother, "please get me four big potatoes." Mark got the biggest potatoes he could find. She said, "Mark, you have been so much help to me. Let's get two ice cream cones."

1. Who went to the store with Grandmother?_____

2. What did Mark push at the store?   _____

3. What meat did Grandmother get for dinner?_____

4. Did Mark get big or little potatoes?   _____

5. How many ice cream cones did they get?_____

DIRECTIONS: Read the story. Then read the five sentences below. Write the missing word in each sentence on the line.

A family of mice lived in the woods. Their home was under a pile of large rocks. In the fall of the year, they began to store food. They gathered corn, nuts, and straw for the long winter months ahead. The little mice worked very hard.

When winter finally came, the days were windy and cold. Snow fell on the ground. It was too cold for the mice to leave their warm home. But they had stored enough food to last them all winter.

After months of cold weather, warm spring days came. The mice were glad to leave their home under the rocks. They ran and played happily in the woods.

1. The story is about a family of _____. (mice   rats   frogs)

2. They lived under some _____. (hay   straw   rocks)

3. The mice began to store their food in the _____. (spring   winter   fall)

4. Corn, nuts, and _____ were gathered for the winter. (straw   water   bees)

5. When _____ came, they ran and played in the woods. (spring   winter   fall)

COMPREHENSION   **E. Recall After Silent Reading**   *4. Sequence*

DIRECTIONS: Read the sentences. Write the answer to each question on the lines.

A. The dog barked at a cat. Then the cat ran up a tree.

   1. What happened first? _____

   _____

   2. Then what happened? _____

   _____

B. Tom's father got a new job. Then the family moved to a new town.

   1. What happened first? _____

   _____

   2. Then what happened? _____

   _____

C. Father got some white paint. Then he painted the house.

   1. What happened first? _____

   _____

   2. Then what happened? _____

   _____

DIRECTIONS: Read the stories. Answer the questions below each story.

A. Nancy was swimming in the pool. Pat jumped into the pool. When she jumped in, she splashed Nancy.

   1. What happened first? _____

   _____

   2. What happened next? _____

   _____

   3. What happened last? _____

   _____

B. Mike put on his roller skates. When he tried to skate, he fell down. Mike got up and tried again.

   1. What happened first? _____

   _____

   2. What happened next? _____

   _____

   3. What happened last? _____

   _____

DIRECTIONS: Read the story. Then read the sentences after the story. Number the sentences from 1 to 4 to show the order in which they happened.

Dan and Timmy wanted to plant a garden. They put the seeds in the ground. Dan got the hose and watered the garden. There were some warm, sunny days. Timmy and Dan went to look at the garden every day. One day they had a big surprise. Little green plants were growing where they had planted seeds!

_____ Dan watered the garden.

_____ The plants came up.

_____ There were some sunny days.

_____ Dan and Timmy planted seeds in the ground.

DIRECTIONS: Read the story. Answer the questions below the story.

Johnny Appleseed was a man who planted many apple trees. He wanted children to have apples to eat and apple trees to climb. First, Johnny would put the black seeds in the ground and cover them with dirt. When the seeds grew into little trees, Johnny would dig up the apple trees. Then he would take the small trees and give them to people to plant in their yards. Every year, when the people ate the apples, they thought of the kind man named Johnny Appleseed.

1. When Johnny wanted to grow an apple tree, what would he do first? _____

_____

2. What would Johnny do next? _____

_____

3. What was the last thing he would do with the small trees?

_____

_____

COMPREHENSION   **E. Recall After Silent Reading**   **4.** *Sequence*

DIRECTIONS: Read the story. Then read the sentences after the story. Number the sentences from 1 to 5 to show the order in which they happened.

Mother and Nan wanted to make a cake. First, they put flour, sugar, eggs, and milk in a bowl. Next, Nan mixed the things in the bowl. Then Mother poured the batter into a pan. Nan put the cake into the oven. When it was ready, Mother took it out of the oven.

_____ Mother poured the batter into a pan.

_____ They put flour, sugar, eggs, and milk in a bowl.

_____ Nan put the cake into the oven.

_____ Nan mixed the batter in the bowl.

_____ Mother took the cake out of the oven.

COMPREHENSION   **F. Distinguishing Real from Imaginary**

TEACHER DIRECTIONS: In a group setting, let the children read each sentence and tell whether it could be real or could not be real. Ask them to tell you how the imaginary statements could be changed to make them possible. Or, have children write "Could be real" or "Could not be real" on the lines.

1.	The cat barked.
2.	The bird made a nest.
3.	"Come here," said the snake.
4.	Mark painted his boat blue.
5.	The cow jumped over the moon.
6.	Ted could eat a horse.
7.	The monkey was at the zoo.

COMPREHENSION   **F. Distinguishing Real from Imaginary**

TEACHER DIRECTIONS: In a group setting, let the children read each sentence and tell whether it could be real or could not be real. Ask them to tell you how the imaginary statements could be changed to make them possible. Or, have children write "Could be real" or "Could not be real" on the lines.

1.	Betty rode her bike to the store.
	_____
2.	"I am strong," said the little tugboat.
	_____
3.	He was as quiet as a mouse.
	_____
4.	He can run as fast as the wind.
	_____
5.	The clock is ticking.
	_____
6.	Mother has some new shoes.
	_____
7.	Fred can ride a horse.
	_____

COMPREHENSION   **F. Distinguishing Real from Imaginary**

DIRECTIONS: Circle the word that will make each sentence true.

1. The   bird / snake   flew up to the tree.

2. Mary went to her house and ate a   banana. / Daddy.

3. The   frog / girl   has a new red dress.

4. Father went outside and picked some   money / apples   from a tree.

5. A   friend / tiger   went to Pat's house to play.

6. Fred ran all the way to the   moon. / school.

7. The   elephant / boy   sat on a wall.

8. "Will you go to the zoo with me?" asked   Sally. / the monkey.

I

COMPREHENSION   **F. Distinguishing Real from Imaginary**

DIRECTIONS: Read the sentences. Below each sentence, circle
<u>Could be real</u> or <u>Could not be real</u>.

1. A witch was flying in the sky on her broom.

   Could be real   Could not be real

2. Mary likes to ride on the school bus with her friends.

   Could be real   Could not be real

3. In the summer many people go swimming.

   Could be real   Could not be real

4. "Good morning. How are you today?" the dog asked the cat.

   Could be real   Could not be real

5. The man in the moon is a friend of mine.

   Could be real   Could not be real

6. The giant pulled up two big trees with his hands.

   Could be real   Could not be real

7. The cowboy won a brown and white horse.

   Could be real   Could not be real

COMPREHENSION   **F. Distinguishing Real from Imaginary**

DIRECTIONS: Read the sentences: Write <u>Could be real</u> or <u>Could not be real</u> on the line below each sentence.

1. Mike is sick in bed with a bad cold.

   _____

2. While playing outside, Mary was as cold as ice.

   _____

3. "You are a nice cat," said the little mouse.

   _____

4. Larry likes to roller skate.

   _____

5. Nancy ate some cookies and drank some milk.

   _____

6. "It's fun to swing from tree to tree," said the monkey.

   _____

7. The ball turned into a rabbit under the magic hat.

   _____

COMPREHENSION   G. Context Clues

DIRECTIONS: Draw a picture in each box to complete the sentence.

1. The Jones family moved into a new blue _____ .

2. Every night Tim's father reads him a _____ with pictures.

3. Sally went outside to the garden to cut _____ to put in a vase.

4. Our dog Dolly had three brown _____ last night.

5. When Fred's house was on fire, a big red _____ came to put out the fire.

6. Dan and Mike went fishing in a _____ in the middle of the pond.

COMPREHENSION   G. Context Clues

DIRECTIONS: Cut out the pictures at the bottom of this page. Paste each picture in the correct box.

1. The [   ] flew to the hive.

2. The nest in the tree was made by a 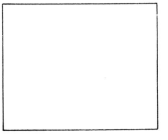 .

3. Tom rode his [   ] .

4. The [   ] at the zoo was very funny.

COMPREHENSION   G. Context Clues

DIRECTIONS: Read each story and circle the correct picture.

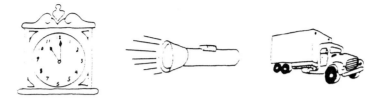

1. One night the car had a flat tire. It was dark
    and Father could not see very well. Tara looked in
    the trunk of the car and got a _____ .

2. Dan went to his grandfather's farm. They
    walked to the chicken house. Dan helped his
    grandfather feed the _____ .

3. Mother went to the store. She wanted to buy
    some food. She took some _____ with her.

4. The boys went to the park. They saw some-
    thing jump in the grass beside the pond. It was a
    small, green _____ .

COMPREHENSION   G. Context Clues

DIRECTIONS: Read the sentences. Draw a line under the sentence in each group that does not belong.

1. Mike went to the pond.

   He put the little boat in the water.

   Sally likes popcorn.

2. Ken wanted to build a snowman.

   It was a very hot day.

   Tom said, "Let's go swimming and get cool."

3. The little red bird built a nest in the tree.

   Nan rode her bike to the park.

   In the spring, four eggs were in the nest.

4. The teacher said, "It's time to go outside and play."

   The children had fun playing outside.

   A rabbit can hop.

5. Sam likes to go to school.

   Joe was very hungry.

   He ate an apple and drank a glass of milk.

6. My family went to the zoo.

   We saw many different animals.

   I can tie my shoes.

COMPREHENSION   G. Context Clues

DIRECTIONS: Read the riddles. Write the word on each line that completes the riddle.

1. I live in the water.

   I have gills.

   I have fins that help me swim.

   I am a _____ . (bat   fish   cat)

2. I have two ears.

   I have four legs.

   I say, "Bow wow."

   I am a _____ . (mouse   dog   frog)

3. I am long and skinny.

   I have no legs.

   I slip and slide on the ground.

   I am a _____ . (monkey   rat   snake)

4. I am very large.

   I have a short tail.

   I have a long nose called a trunk.

   I am an _____ . (elephant   ant   egg)

5. I am very small.

   I like to eat food at picnics.

   If I bite you, it will sting.

   I am an _____ . (goat   egg   ant)

COMPREHENSION   H. Appropriate Title

DIRECTIONS: Color the picture below. Then cut out the best title for the picture at the bottom of this page. Paste the title in the box above the picture.

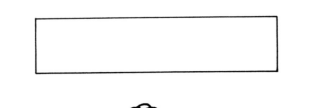

The Funny Clown   A New Puppy

COMPREHENSION   H. Appropriate Title

DIRECTIONS: Draw a line from each title to the correct sentence.

Part A

Titles	Sentences
1. The Apple Tree	Baby bears are born in the spring.
2. Baby Bears	We have a big apple tree.
3. The Snowman	John had a surprise birthday party.
4. Our Park	Our class made a big snowman.
5. Happy Birthday!	Our park is a fun place to go to.

Part B

Titles	Sentences
1. Kim and Jan	Kim and Jan are sisters.
2. A Funny Puppy	Billy and I went to the toy store.
3. At the Toy Store	Our class went to the zoo.
4. The Train	Andy got a new puppy named Spot.
5. Our Trip to the Zoo	We rode the train to grandmother's house.

I

COMPREHENSION   H. Appropriate Title

DIRECTIONS: Read the stories. Put an X by the best title for each story.

1.   Tim's class visited the police station. Officer Thomas showed them around the station. He told them about how policemen and policewomen help people. He answered the questions the children asked. Before the class left, he let each child wear his police hat.

_____ The Fire Station

_____ A Trip to the Police Station

_____ Tim and His Friends

2.   Kay's father came home with a box. "Kay," said Father, "I have a surprise for you." The box had holes in the top of it. Kay heard something move inside. Father smiled and said, "Open the box. Your surprise wants to get out." Kay took the top off the box. A cute brown puppy jumped out. "Thank you, Father!" said Kay. "This is a very nice surprise!"

_____ Kay and Mother

_____ A Birthday Party

_____ A Surprise for Kay

Name: _____ Date: _____

COMPREHENSION   H. Appropriate Title

DIRECTIONS: Read the story and the title below the story. Put an X by the two titles that could be used for the story.

"Carlos," said the teacher, "you may paint a picture about anything you want today." Carlos painted a picture of his father. His father wore brown pants and a blue shirt. Then he painted his mother in a pretty red dress with red shoes. Next to his mother, he painted a picture of his baby sister. She was playing in a sandbox. Carlos also painted a picture of himself riding his bike. He wrote "My Family" across the top of his picture. Carlos said, "I like my picture. I will take it home and put it on the living room wall."

_____ Carlos and His Teacher

_____ Father and Mother Go Shopping

_____ A Family Picture

_____ Carlos Gets a New Bike

_____ Carlos Paints a Picture

I   233

COMPREHENSION   H. Appropriate Title

DIRECTIONS: Read the stories. Write a title for each story on the line above it.

1.   _____

Dogs have many different kinds of hair. Some dogs have long hair. Other dogs have short hair. The hair of a dog is like a coat that the dog wears all the time. In the winter, the hair of a dog gets thicker to help keep it warm. Dogs with long hair need to have their hair clipped in the summer so they will not become too hot.

2.   _____

Wind is air that moves very fast. You cannot see the wind, but you can see things being pushed by it. Wind makes many things move—like leaves, flags, and dust. Have you ever watched the wind push a sailboat? Even though no one has ever seen the wind, it is very real.

COMPREHENSION   **I. Relating Story Content to Own Experiences**

DIRECTIONS: Cut out each word and paste it in the box by the correct picture.

COMPREHENSION   I. Relating Story Content to Own Experiences

DIRECTIONS: Read the story. Draw a picture at the bottom of this sheet about something that happened to you that made you unhappy.

It was a very hot day. Ned wanted something cold to eat. "Mother," said Ned, "may I go to the store and get some ice cream?" "Yes, but I want you to take your little brother with you," answered Mother. "I know that he would like some ice cream, too." Ted was very unhappy. He did not want to take his little brother with him. "I won't go if he has to go!" said Ted. "I will stay home!"

Name: _____ Date: _____

DIRECTIONS: Draw a picture about something that happened to you that made you feel like the word in the box. Tell your teacher what happened that made you feel the way you did.

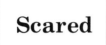

Scared

DIRECTIONS: Read the story. Answer the questions below the story.

Ted wanted a pet. "Mother," said Ted, "may I have a cat or a dog?" "No," said Mother. "Pets need a lot of care. You must feed them every day. You must make sure they have water to drink. When they get dirty, you must wash them. Pets also need someone to take the time to play with them." Ted looked very sad. "Ted," said Mother, "when you are a little older, you may get a pet."

1. Do you have a pet? _____

2. Have you ever wanted a pet that you could not have?

_____

3. How would you feel if you were Ted? _____

4. Would you like to help take care of a pet? _____

5. If you could have any pet, what would you want?

_____

6. Have you ever had to wait until you were older to own something? _____

7. If so, what was it? _____

COMPREHENSION   I. Relating Story Content to Own Experiences

DIRECTIONS: Read the story. Write what you would do if you were in Carlos's class.

A new boy moved to town. He was in the same class as Carlos. His desk was next to Carlos's desk. The new boy was from another country. When he talked he sounded different. He did not know how to play the games that Carlos and his friends played. None of the children wanted to talk to him or play with him. The new boy looked very sad.

_____

_____

_____

_____

_____

Answer Key

VOCABULARY

A. Word Recognition

1. Upper- and lower-case letters at beginning

Page 17
1. Dog, dog
2. Hog, hog
3. Log log
4. Frog, frog

Page 18

Part A:
1. Ping, ping
2. ring, Ring
3. King, king
4. Ding, ding
5. swing, Swing

Part B:
6. look, Look
7. Hook, hook
8. cook, Cook
9. Took, took
10. brook, Brook

Page 19
1. It, it
2. Bat, bat
3. Get, get
4. Lip, lip
5. Red, red
6. Dig, dig
7. Pen, pen
8. Lay, lay
9. Moon, moon
10. Jump, jump
11. Kick, kick
12. Sing, sing

Page 20 An X should appear on boxes 3, 4, 6, 7, 8, 10, 12.

Page 21
1. yet, Yet
2. ray, Ray
3. lid, Lid
4. how, How
5. pig, Pig
6. got, Got
7. wed, Wed
8. van, Van
9. joy, Joy
10. sit, Sit
11. tall, Tall
12. zip, Zip

Page 22
1. jump
2. heat
3. coat
4. make
5. dear
6. ride
7. bent
8. kind
9. five
10. noon

2. Names of letters in sequence

Page 23

Part A:
1. B
2. D
3. N
4. F
5. I
6. P
7. K
8. Y
9. X

Part B:
10. K
11. U
12. E
13. P
14. C
15. R
16. Y
17. H
18. X

Page 24
1. B
2. D
3. Z
4. V
5. J
6. G
7. X
8. A
9. H
10. N
11. N
12. S
13. F
14. D
15. M

Page 25
1. C
2. V
3. E
4. V
5. Q
6. C
7. H
8. L
9. P
10. U
11. Z
12. I
13. L
14. Q

Page 26
1. C, E, G, J, L, P, S, W, Z
2. A, C, D, F, H, I, K, M, N, Q, R, T, V, X, Y

Answer Key

Page 27	1. C 2. M 3. T, V

Page 28   1. Z   2. G, J   3. Q

Page 29   C, F, H, K, N, Q, S, V, X, Z

3.   *Words in preprimers and primers*

Page 30   Pictures will vary.

Page 31   Pictures will vary.

Page 32   Pictures will vary.

Page 33
1. table
2. toy
3. pie
4. cake

Page 34
1. girl
2. kitten
3. cookies
4. bed

Page 35
1. can
2. two
3. man
4. boat
5. dish
6. tree

Page 36
1. ball
2. rabbit
3. apple
4. mitten
5. fish
6. house

Page 37
1. boy
2. one
3. car
4. TV
5. dog
6. saw

WORD ANALYSIS

A.   *Sound-Symbol Associations*

1.   *Associates consonant sounds to letters:*

Page 54
b—boat, back
c—cane, cold
d—dad, dance, do
f—flag, fly
g—go, goat
m—me, milk, music

Page 55
n—nut, nail
p—pet, pick
q—queen, quiet
r—rat, run, rope
s—sand, sun
h—hot, horse, hug

Page 56
h—horse, hut
j—jacks, just
k—kite, keg
l—less, love
m—me, milk, music
b—ball, back

Page 57
t—toe, tall, the
v—vote, voice
w—week, wet, who
x—x-ray, xylophone
y—you, young
z—zoo, zebra

Page 58   balloon, bell, boat, baby, baseball bat

Page 59   coat, car, cup, cap, cake, cow

Page 60   desk, doll, donut, dinosaur, doctor

Page 61   fish, foot, fire, feather, finger

Page 62   groceries, grapes, goat, gum, guitar, gate

Page 63   hat, heart, horse, hammer, hippopotamus, house

Page 64   jacks, jeep, jump rope, jacket, jelly

Page 65   kite, kangaroo, key, king, kitchen

Page 66   lamp, lion, lipstick, ladder, lemon

Page 67   man, mousetrap, mitten, money, mask, match

Page 68   nut, newspaper, needle, necklace, nest

Page 69   pan, pen, pencil, penny, pear

Page 70   quilt, question mark, quarter

Page 71   rope, rabbit, ring, robot, rake

Page 72   sandwich, sock, sink, sailor, six, scissors

Page 73   table, turkey, tire, two, tiger, top

Page 74   vest, violin, vacuum cleaner, volcano, valentine

Page 75   worm, web, wagon, watermelon, watch, wig

Page 76   yarn, yacht, yard, yawn, yolk

Page 77   zebra, zero, zipper, zigzag

Page 78
1. boat, ball
2. cat, coat
3. dog, donut
4. fan, foot
5. gum, girl

Page 79
1. horse, helicopter
2. jet, jeep
3. king, key
4. ladder, lock
5. money, moon

Page 80
1. net, nine
2. pie, pumpkin
3. queen, question
4. ring, rake
5. sailor, six

Page 81
1. ten, tiger
2. vest, violin
3. watch, witch
4. yawn, yo-yo
5. zebra, zipper

2.   *Names letters to represent consonant sounds heard in:*

a.   *Initial position*

Page 82
1. ballerina
2. house
3. ring
4. ten
5. zipper

Page 83
1. yarn
2. mitten
3. doll
4. vest
5. kitchen

Page 84
1. coat
2. jeep
3. needle
4. sailor
5. walrus

Page 85
1. lion
2. quarter
3. flag
4. pig
5. gum

Page 86
1. b
2. h
3. l
4. d
5. w

Page 87
1. j
2. r
3. c
4. t
5. p
6. n
7. f
8. s
9. w
10. g

b. *Final position*

Page 88	1. web	4. bed
	2. bank	5. dog
	3. tail	

Page 89	1. glass	4. beehive
	2. calf	5. sneeze
	3. drum	

Page 90	1. hat	4. bear
	2. bell	5. man
	3. lamp	

Page 91	1. m	6. g
	2. t	7. s
	3. n	8. p
	4. d	9. m
	5. b	10. f

Page 92	1. cat	6. wood
	2. man	7. car
	3. cup	8. sun
	4. rug	9. bus
	5. bell	

c. *Medial position*

Page 93	1. mitten	4. seven
	2. paper	5. cactus
	3. crayon	

Page 94	1. puzzle	4. grasshopper
	2. shadow	5. basket
	3. banjo	

Page 95	1. b	4. l
	2. k	5. n
	3. g	6. c

Page 96	1. t	4. v
	2. h	5. p
	3. f	6. m

3. *Discriminates between words using:*
a. *Initial letter cues*

| **Page 97** | 1. net | 3. well |
| | 2. zoo | 4. rat |

Page 98	1. dog	4. queen
	2. fan	5. pig
	3. vest	

Page 99	1. mitten	4. nail
	2. bee	5. tent
	3. hat	

Page 100	1. cat	6. king
	2. jet	7. lock
	3. soap	8. house
	4. yarn	9. goat
	5. pen	10. fire

b. *Final letter cues*

| **Page 101** | 1. pig | 3. six |
| | 2. swim | 4. glass |

Page 102	1. rock	4. nail
	2. bug	5. chair
	3. horse	

Page 103	1. foot	4. cow
	2. ten	5. sled
	3. bib	

Page 104	1. flag	6. bird
	2. drum	7. map
	3. coat	8. fox
	4. girl	9. jet
	5. van	10. bus

4. *Associates sounds to digraphs*

Page 105	shoe, sheep, shell, ship, shovel, shirt
Page 106	whistle, whale, wheat, whip
Page 107	thumb, third, throw, thread, thimble
Page 108	chicken, chalk, chair, church, chimney, chipmunk

Page 109	1. sh	6. wh
	2. th	7. ch
	3. sh	8. sh
	4. wh	9. th
	5. ch	

5. *Associates sounds to two-letter blends*

Page 110	1. st	6. bl
	2. bl	7. bl
	3. st	8. pl
	4. pl	9. pl
	5. st	

| **Page 111** | 1. tray, train, tree, triangle |
| | 2. fruit, frame, frown, freckles |

Page 112	1. gl	6. gl
	2. fl	7. cl
	3. cl	8. gl
	4. fl	9. fl
	5. cl	

| **Page 113** | 1. grapes, grandfather, grass, groceries |
| | 2. spool, spider, spot, sponge |

Page 114	1. smoke, smell
	2. sneeze, snake, snowman
	3. swing, swim, sweep

Page 115	1. bread, bridge
	2. grow, grape
	3. slide, sled
	4. stop, star
	5. blink, block
	6. plate, pliers
	7. brick, bring
	8. grade, grape
	9. slap, sleep
	10. step, stack

Page 116	1. pl	6. st
	2. bl	7. st
	3. pl	8. pl
	4. bl	9. bl
	5. st	

Answer Key

Page 117
1. trampoline, tray
2. fruit, frog
3. flag, flashlight
4. clown, cloud
5. globe, glove

Page 118
1. sm	6. gr
2. sp	7. gr
3. sp	8. gr
4. sp	9. sm
5. sm	

Page 119
1. snowman, snail
2. swim, sweater
3. brush, broom
4. grandfather, groundhog
5. slide, sleep

6. *Knows that the letters* a, e, i, o, u, *and combinations of these can represent several different sounds*

Page 120 Pictures circled: bat, hand, map, man, rat, pan
Pictures with an X: plate, skates, cake, whale

Page 121 Pictures circled: desk, pen, sled, bread, belt, nest
Pictures with an X: jeep, queen, bee, teeth

Page 122 Pictures circled: fish, pin, ship, lips
Pictures with an X: mice, kite, pipe, pie, tie, knife

Page 123 Column A: mop, rock, dog, box, blocks, dock
Column B: soap, note, toe, bone, goat, rose

Page 124 Pictures circled: rug, nut, bus, drum, cup
Pictures with an X: tube, flute, fruit, tuba, suit

Page 125
1. u	7. u
2. e	8. a
3. i	9. i
4. e	10. o
5. a	11. o
6. a	12. e

Page 126
1. o	7. i
2. e	8. o
3. a	9. o
4. u	10. o
5. a	11. e
6. i	12. u

B. *Structural Analysis*

1. *Knows endings*

a. ed *sound as "ed" in* wanted

Page 127
1. painted	6. dusted
2. salted	7. shouted
3. skated	10. wanted
5. heated	

Page 128
1. wanted	5. skated
2. started	6. salted
3. planted	7. painted
4. needed	8. shouted

Page 129
1. wanted	5. hunted
2. started	6. needed
3. planted	7. heated
4. shouted	8. pasted

Page 130
1. Yes	6. Yes
2. No	7. No
3. Yes	8. Yes
4. No	9. No
5. No	10. Yes

b. ed *sound as "d" in* moved

Page 131
1. poured	5. sawed
2. colored	7. pulled
3. mowed	8. climbed

Page 132
1. purred	5. called
2. poured	6. peeled
3. pulled	7. watered
4. showed	8. played

Page 133
1. showed	6. killed
2. filled	7. played
3. purred	8. mowed
4. poured	9. lived
5. stayed	

Page 134
1. Yes	6. No
2. Yes	7. Yes
3. No	8. No
4. No	9. Yes
5. Yes	10. Yes

c. ed *sound as "t" in* linked

Page 135
2. splashed	7. washed
3. skipped	8. walked
4. kicked	9. backed
5. hopped	10. fixed

Page 136
1. worked	5. looked
2. jumped	6. dropped
3. pushed	7. walked
4. fixed	8. splashed

Page 137 Part A:
1. tricked	5. cooked
2. jumped	7. kicked
4. splashed	8. looked

Part B:
2. helped	8. pushed
4. hopped	10. mopped
6. worked	

Page 138
1. Yes	6. Yes
2. No	7. No
3. Yes	8. Yes
4. Yes	9. No
5. No	10. No

2.   *Recognizes compound words*

Page 139   1. doghouse   3. fishhook
2. toothbrush   4. raincoat

Page 140   1. cowboy   4. railroad
2. airplane   5. without
3. goldfish

Page 141   1. dollhouse   5. playground
2. football   6. birthday
3. policeman   7. sidewalk
4. grandmother

Page 142   1. doorbell   5. firemen
2. sunlight   6. housework
3. mailbox   7. raindrops
4. treehouse

Page 143   1. in to   6. snow man
2. cow girl   7. moon light
3. foot ball   8. bed room
4. some thing   9. play house
5. air plane   10. rail road

Page 144   1. side walk   6. grand mother
2. with out   7. after noon
3. sun light   8. butter milk
4. birth day   9. sun flower
5. can not   10. police man

3.   *Knows common word families*

Page 145   Answers are not limited to these:
1. p, t, f   6. s, f, p, b
2. w, t, s, f   7. p, s, l
3. s, p, t, h, l 8. p, f, s, w
4. s, f, c, h   9. s, w, fl, r
5. h, s, p

Page 146   Answers are not limited to these:
1. p, f, w, b   6. sh, sl, fl, h, l
2. t, f, h, c   7. w, f, d
3. sl, f, l, b   8. h, s, p
4. P, S, t, sl   9. c, h, m, p, t, sh
5. p, sh, h, n, r

Page 147   Answers are not limited to these:
1. s, h, p   7. d, h, l, n, s
2. h, t, l, b   8. b, f, s, t
3. b, c, f, h, m 9. l, d, tr
4. d, f, sw, w   10. f, p, w, g
5. s, h, tr   11. b, c, f, l
6. t, r, b, l, p 12. d, k, p, r, s

Page 148   Answers are not limited to these:
1. f, t   9. h, t
2. s, t   10. l, c, p
3. s, pr   11. m, r
4. b, f   12. b, r
5. l, t   13. t, m
6. d, tr, c   14. b, l
7. w, d   15. s, h
8. f, l, m

C.   *Word Form Clues*

1.   *Recognizes upper- and lower-case letters*

Page 149   Upper-case letters: B, F, W, H, J, S, V, D, L, A, T, C, Q, M, R, E, I, G, Y, O, U
Lower-case letters: u, d, c, l, y, h, m, s, q, z, b, x, f, t, k, n, v, p, a, r, e

Page 150   1. Red   9. name
2. Boy   10. goat
3. can   11. Queen
4. It   12. Sit
5. mat   13. tree
6. Walk   14. vest
7. funny   15. Apple
8. Jump

Page 151
Part A.   Upper-case letters: R, B, S, K, T, L, E, F, W, O, H, P, Y, D, Q, Z
Part B.   Lower-case letters: j, n, y, k, o, d, z, c, l, p, t, d, m, e, f

Page 152   1. Dan   6. Queen
2. Tiger   7. Gary, Ricky
3. Carlos, I   8. Mark
4. Mike   9. Ted, I
5. Nan, I   10. Jim, Will

Page 153   1. Lower-case letters: a, c, e, m, o, p, w, x, n
2. Upper-case letters: H, P, E, W, O, K, A, F, C, Z, T, R, N, D
3. Match: j-J, K-k, g-G, y-Y, p-P, i-I, f-F, w-W, u-U, C-c, l-L, n-N

Page 154   Box A: r, a, e, h, g, l, w, p, d, y, c
Box B: M, F, O, W, J, A, X, T, M, G, S

Page 155
Part A.   Upper case letters: F, L, S, B, H, G, C, K, U, T, N, R, V, I, H
Part B.   Lower case letters:
1. s, t, b, w   4. o, f, l, q
2. m, k, c, n   5. g, p, h, j
3. y, d, i, e   6. r, v, x, a

2.   *Recognizes words of different length*

Page 156   1. football   7. bicycle
2. hippopotamus 8. tricycle
3. jacket   9. table
4. monkey   10. grapes
5. kitten   11. pencil
6. cookies   12. butter

Page 157   1. typewriter   7. apple
2. telephone   8. pineapple
3. television   9. necklace
4. piano   10. curtains
5. lipstick   11. basket
6. flowers   12. tiger

Page 158   1. B   5. A
2. A   6. A
3. B   7. B
4. A   8. B

Answer Key

Page 159
1. 1	5. 2
2. 2	6. 1
3. 1	7. 2
4. 2	8. 2

3. *Recognizes words with double letters*

Page 160
1. ball	5. door
2. kitten	6. Daddy
3. bee	7. book
4. rabbit	8. bell

Page 161   pretty, book, cook, doll, ball, kitten, apple, fall, poppy, green, fell

Page 162
1. dress	6. puppy
2. hook	7. three
3. Betty	8. smell
4. jeep	9. bunny
5. zoo	10. need

Page 163   Column A: tall, penny, seed, took, Larry, sleep, pill
Column B: soon, little, apple, tennis, yellow, tree, room, puppy

COMPREHENSION

A. *Symbolic Representation*

Page 164
1. horse	4. stove
2. boat	5. lamp
3. girl	6. truck

Descriptions of each picture will vary.

Page 165   Pictures and words will vary.

Page 166   Pictures will vary.

Page 167
1. cat	3. bed
2. pie	4. girl

Page 168
1. rabbit	3. puppy
2. tree	4. ball

Page 169   Children should be able to dramatize the words on the flashcards.

B. *Following Printed Directions*

Page 170
1. red balloon	4. yellow rectangle
2. black dog	5. green circle
3. blue triangle	

Page 171   1. ☆   3. ↑

2. 1 2 <u>3</u> 4 5   4.

Page 172   1. Ⓖ   4. E E / E E

2. △ (X)   5. 5 _____ 6

3. ‖‖‖

Page 173   1. <u>A</u>   4. 1 2 ③ 4 5 6 7 8 9 10

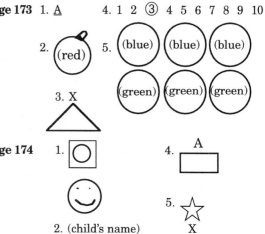

2. (red)   5. (blue) (blue) (blue) / (green) (green) (green)

3. X △

Page 174   1. ▢○   4. ▭ A

2. ☺ (child's name)   5. ☆ X

3. ① 2 3 4 <u>5</u> 6 7

C. *Drawing Conclusions*

Page 175
1. birthday	4. yes
2. Sam	5. cake
3. seven years old	6. inside

Page 176
1. sandwich	4. swing
2. car	5. mask
3. star	

Page 177
1. airplane	3. apple
2. ball	4. umbrella

Page 178
1. hurt	4. sick
2. sad	5. tired
3. hungry	

Page 179
1. dog	3. fish
2. airplane (jet)	4. sun

D. *Recall from Stories Read Aloud*

1. *Main idea*

Page 180   Pictures will vary.

Page 181   1. Dan wanted one of Tom's puppies.
3. Tim and Sam saw many animals at the zoo.

Page 182   2. Bill Helps on the Farm
2. A Big Fish

Page 183   1. Mike and Joe liked to play baseball.
2. Sue likes to go to the library.
3. Fred had a birthday party.

Page 184   2. We need the heat and the light from the sun to live.
1. You can make new colors by mixing different colors of paint.

2. *Characters*

Page 185
1. Jan Smith	3. Mary Martin
2. Sherry Jones	

Page 186
1. Mark
2. Susie
3. Kevin
4. Brad
5. Nan's
6. Sally
7. Uncle Joe

Page 187 Picture of a frog, a mouse, and an ant will vary.

Page 188
1. Mrs. Green
2. Betsy
3. Carla

Page 189
1. Mr. Parks
2. Fred, Mark
3. Mr. Young
4. Mark

3. Details

Page 190
1. truck
2. Hill Elementary School
3. Wednesday
4. red
5. two
6. farm
7. three

Page 191
1. happy face
2. sad face
3. sad face
4. happy face
5. happy face

Page 192 Pictures will vary, but should include:
1. sunny day
2. bird
3. cat
4. baby brother

Page 193
1. library
2. two
3. Fast Cars
4. cookbook
5. The Three Little Pigs
6. Mrs. Brown

Page 194
1. food
2. roots
3. water
4. leaves
5. gas

4. Sequence

Page 195 A.
1. Tom went to the park.
2. He went to Fred's house.

B.
1. Mary read a book.
2. She went outside to play.

C.
1. Sam cleaned his room.
2. He did his homework.

Page 196
1. Tim and Mother put the dishes on the table.
2. They cooked the food.
3. Tim and Mother put the food on the table.

Page 197
1. shells
2. seaweed
3. a piece of wood

Page 198
1. Kim went riding on her bike.
2. Kim saw a bird building its nest.
3. She saw Mr. Chin mowing his grass.
4. She saw some children playing ball.

Page 199
1. Carol went to visit the dentist.
2. Dr. Jones cleaned Carol's teeth.
3. The dentist gave Carol a new toothbrush.

4. Dr. Jones showed Carol how to brush her teeth.
5. Dr. Jones told Carol that she had a pretty smile.

E. Recall After Silent Reading

1. Main idea

Page 200 Pictures will vary.

Page 201
1. Sue got a new bicycle for her birthday.
2. Grandfather and Dan went to the zoo.
3. Joe and Buddy went fishing.

Page 202
1. At the Playhouse
2. A Surprise for Andy

Page 203
3. Tom went to his grandfather's farm.
2. Kim does many things at school.

Page 204
3. If you were in a rocket in space, you could see many interesting things.

2. Characters

Page 205
1. Nan
2. Mark
3. Tim
4. Sam
5. Fred
6. Carl
7. Ned

Page 206
1. Sammy
2. Mary and Cathy
3. Fred
4. Sammy and Ken

Page 207
1. Mr. Lopez
2. Ben
3. Nicky
4. Mark
5. Pedro

Page 208
1. sad face
2. sad face
3. happy face
4. happy face
5. sad face
6. happy face

Page 209
1. Mother
2. Grandfather
3. Daddy
4. Pat's big brother
5. Aunt Nell
6. Pat

3. Details

Page 210
1. snake
2. seven years old
3. Saturday
4. two
5. Main Street
6. card
7. Mark Brown

Page 211
1. basketball
2. three
3. ball and bat
4. under a tree

Page 212
1. at her house
2. seven years old
3. a small book
4. red

Page 213
1. Mark
2. shopping cart
3. ham
4. big
5. two

Page 214
1. mice
2. rocks
3. fall
4. straw
5. spring

Answer Key

4. Sequence

Page 215 A.
    1. The dog barked at a cat.
    2. The cat ran up a tree.
    B.
    1. Tom's father got a new job.
    2. The family moved to a new town.
    C.
    1. Father got some white paint.
    2. He painted the house.

Page 216 A.
    1. Nancy was swimming.
    2. Pat jumped into the pool.
    3. Pat splashed Nancy.
    B.
    1. Mike put on his roller skates.
    2. He fell down.
    3. He tried to skate again.

Page 217
1. Dan and Timmy planted seeds in the ground.
2. Dan watered the garden.
3. There were some sunny days.
4. The plants came up.

Page 218
1. He put the seeds in the ground and covered them with dirt.
2. He dug up the small trees.
3. He gave them to people to plant.

Page 219
1. They put flour, sugar, eggs, and milk in a bowl.
2. Nan mixed the batter in the bowl.
3. Mother poured the batter into a pan.
4. Nan put the cake into the oven.
5. Mother took the cake out of the oven.

F. Distinguishing Real from Imaginary

Page 220
1. Could not be real
2. Could be real
3. Could not be real
4. Could be real
5. Could not be real
6. Could not be real
7. Could be real

Page 221
1. Could be real
2. Could not be real
3. Could be real
4. Could not be real
5. Could be real
6. Could be real
7. Could be real

Page 222
1. bird
2. banana
3. girl
4. apples
5. friend
6. school
7. boy
8. Sally

Page 223
1. Could not be real
2. Could be real
3. Could be real
4. Could not be real
5. Could not be real
6. Could not be real
7. Could be real

Page 224
1. Could be real
2. Could not be real
3. Could not be real
4. Could be real

5. Could be real
6. Could not be real
7. Could not be real

G. Context Clues

Page 225 Pictures will vary, but should include:
1. house, trailer, or apartment
2. book
3. flowers
4. puppies
5. fire truck
6. boat

Page 226
1. bee
2. bird
3. bicycle
4. monkey

Page 227
1. flashlight
2. chickens
3. money
4. grasshopper

Page 228
1. Sally likes popcorn.
2. Ken wanted to build a snowman.
3. Nan rode her bike to the park.
4. A rabbit can hop.
5. Sam likes to go to school.
6. I can tie my shoes.

Page 229
1. fish
2. dog
3. snake
4. elephant
5. ant

H. Appropriate Title

Page 230 The Funny Clown

Page 231 Part A.
1. We have a big apple tree.
2. Baby bears are born in the spring.
3. Our class made a big snowman.
4. Our park is a fun place to go to.
5. John had a surprise birthday party.

Part B.
1. Kim and Jan are sisters.
2. Andy got a new puppy named Spot.
3. Billy and I went to the toy store.
4. We rode the train to grandmother's house.
5. Our class went to the zoo.

Page 232
1. A Trip to the Police Station
2. A Surprise for Kay

Page 233 A Family Picture
Carlos Paints a Picture

Page 234 Titles will vary.

I. Relating Story Content to Own Experiences

Page 235
1. mad
2. sleepy
3. happy
4. sad

Page 236 Pictures will vary.

Page 237 Pictures and answers will vary.

Page 238 Answers will vary.

Page 239 Answers will vary.

Class Record of Reading Skills
FIRST LEVEL

On the following pages you will find copies of a Class Record of Reading Skills: FIRST LEVEL. This can be used to record the progress of your entire class or an individual child in mastering the specific skills at the First Level.

    The Class Record can help you identify groups of students who need instruction in a particular skill and to assess the relative strengths and levels of individual students. The Class Record can also be used in conferences with administrators, parents, and students to discuss reading skills progress.

Name of Teacher: _____

CLASS RECORD OF
READING SKILLS
FIRST LEVEL

Student Names

Column headers (read vertically):

- I. Vocabulary:
- A. Word Recognition
  - 1. Recognizes words with both upper- and lower-case letters at beginning
  - 2. Knows names of letters in sequence
  - 3. Is able to identify in various settings words usually found in preprimers and primers
- II. Word Analysis:
- A. Sound-symbol Association
  - 1. Associates consonant sounds
  - 2. Names letters to represent consonant sounds
    - a. Initial position
    - b. Final position
    - c. Medial position
  - 3. Discriminates between words
    - a. Initial letter cues
    - b. Final letter cues
  - 4. Associates sounds to digraphs
  - 5. Associates sounds to two-letter blends
  - 6. Knows that the letters a, e, i, o, u, and combinations of these can represent several different sounds
- B. Structural Analysis
  - 1. Knows endings
    - a. ed sound as "ed" in wanted
    - b. ed sound as "d" in moved
    - c. ed sound as "t" in liked
  - 2. Recognizes compound words
  - 3. Knows common word families
- C. Word Form Clues
  - 1. Recognizes upper- and lower-case letters

2. Recognizes words of different length
3. Recognizes words with double letters
III. Comprehension
A. Understands that printed symbols represent objects or actions
B. Can follow printed directions
C. Can draw conclusions from given facts
D. Can recall from stories read aloud:
1. Main idea
2. Names of characters
3. Important details
4. Stated sequence
E. Can recall after silent reading:
1. Main idea
2. Names of characters
3. Important details
4. Stated sequence
F. Can distinguish between real and imaginary events
G. Uses context clues in word attack
H. Can suggest or select an appropriate title for a story
I. Can relate story content to own experiences
IV. Oral and Silent Reading Skills
A. Oral Reading
1. Uses correct pronunciation
2. Uses correct phrasing (not word-by-word)
3. Uses proper voice intonation to give meaning
4. Has good posture and handles book appropriately
5. Understands simple punctuation
   a. Period
   b. Comma
   c. Question mark
   d. Exclamation mark
B. Silent Reading
1. Reads without vocalization
2. Reads without head movements